Psychology, Society, and Subjectivity

One result of the European student movements of the late 1960s was a critique of the mainstream, bourgeois social sciences. They were seen as irrelevant to the real needs of ordinary people and as practically and ideologically supporting oppression.

The discussions around psychology in Berlin at the time became increasingly focused on whether the discipline could in fact be reformed. Some insisted that any form of institutionalized social science was necessarily oppressive, while others remained optimistic about the possibilities for an emancipatory science. Among the latter was a group under the leadership of Klaus Holzkamp at the Free University who undertook an intensive critique of psychology with a view to identifying and correcting its theoretical and methodological problems and thus laying the groundwork for a genuine 'critical' psychology.

Psychology, Society, and Subjectivity relates the history of this development, the nature of the group's critique, its reconstruction of psychology, and its implications for psychological thought and practice. It will be of interest to anyone keen on making psychology more relevant to our lives.

Charles Tolman is Professor of Psychology at the University of Victoria, Canada. He is the editor of *Positivism in Psychology* (1991) and (with Wolfgang Maiers) *Critical Psychology* (1991).

Critical Psychology
Series editors

John Broughton
Columbia University, New York

David Ingleby
Vakgroep KPG, Utrecht

Valerie Walkerdine
Goldsmiths' College, London

Since the 1960s there has been widespread disaffection with traditional approaches in psychology, and talk of a 'crisis' has been endemic. At the same time, psychology has encountered influential contemporary movements such as feminism, neo-marxism, post-structuralism and post-modernism. In this climate, various forms of 'critical psychology' have developed vigorously.

Unfortunately, such work – drawing as it does on unfamiliar intellectual traditions – is often difficult to assimilate. The aim of the Critical Psychology series is to make this exciting new body of work readily accessible to students and teachers of psychology, as well as presenting the more psychological aspects of this work to a wider social scientific audience. Specially commissioned works from leading critical writers will demonstrate the relevance of their new approaches to a wide range of current social issues.

Titles in the series include:

Psychology, Society, and Subjectivity

An Introduction to German Critical Psychology

Charles W. Tolman

London and New York

First published 1994
by Routledge
11 New Fetter Lane, London EC4P 4EE

Simultaneously published in the USA and Canada
by Routledge
29 West 35th Street, New York, NY 10001

© 1994 Charles W. Tolman

Typeset in Times by LaserScript, Mitcham, Surrey
Printed and bound in Great Britain by
Mackays of Chatham PLC, Chatham, Kent

British Library Cataloguing in Publication Data
A catalogue record for this book is available from the British Library

Library of Congress Cataloging in Publication Data
A catalogue record for this book has been requested

ISBN 0–415–08975–1 (hbk)
ISBN 0–415–08976–X (pbk)

Contents

Preface

Is a *science* of the human subject possible? This is not a new question. Its roots are as old as the mind–body problem itself, but it first came noticeably to the surface with the development of a self-conscious social science. It thus lay at the heart of nineteenth-century debates around the natural sciences (*Naturwissenschaften*) and the mental sciences (*Geisteswissenschaften*). This debate had its focus in Germany, where the answer given to our question by such prominent figures as Wilhelm Wundt, Wilhelm Dilthey, and Edmund Husserl was an emphatic 'Yes!'. They insisted that the human subject, being something quite special in nature, required its own science. For Wundt this was the *Völkerpsychologie*; for Dilthey it was *hermeneutics*, while for Husserl it was *phenomenology*. Each was marked both by a definition of its subject matter as distinct from that of the natural sciences, and by one or more methods that were also distinct and generally not 'experimental' in the usual sense of the term.

For some German but especially British and American philosophers, psychologists, and social scientists the answer to the question was less univocal. It could be 'yes', but only under certain conditions. The main one was a willingness to *reduce* the seemingly distinctive qualities of the human subject to the more familiar processes of physics, chemistry, and physiology. The answer was 'no' for some who denied that there was anything worth reducing in the first place. This is also a species of reductive answer and it helps to reveal an important ambivalence in reductionism. Nowhere is this more apparent than in John B. Watson's attitudes towards consciousness. Unable to decide for himself which form of reductionism was more appropriate, he sometimes denied outright the existence of anything that could be called 'consciousness', while at other times he treated it as something that could be equated to the use of language, which, in turn, was understood as conditioned muscular movements. Watson exhibited yet a third position, again reflecting the fundamental ambivalence of his position: consciousness may exist, but it was of no concern to science. This view is actually a product of the other two and shows up the hidden dualist metaphysics that reductionism preserves while claiming to repudiate.

There is, of course, something right about both the German solution and the reductionist one. The hermeneuticist, for example, does not deny the physical and physiological bases of language and meaning. And most reductionisms, except perhaps for some of the sillier forms that only an isolated few take seriously, must allow that there is something to be reduced.

As we shall see, German Critical Psychology takes a *synthetic* view of the matter. It seeks to affirm the uniqueness of the human subject because it is precisely *subjectivity* that is at stake in the politics of human well-being. It is an obvious fact of experience that we as human beings organize ourselves into societal arrangements for the purpose of satisfying human needs; that in the course of this we actually create new needs and new satisfactions, and consequently new societal arrangements; and that *history* is something more than mere evolution. At the heart of facts like these lies subjectivity. Human beings truly are *subjects* of their own existences and histories in ways that other animals appear not to be. This, then, cannot be denied or circumvented by any social science with the least pretension to scientific adequateness: on the contrary, subjectivity must constitute the very subject matter and epistemic standpoint of social science.

At the same time, human beings were not simply dropped here out of space. We are biological beings who belong to the natural world and many of the needs we seek to satisfy through our societal arrangements reflect this. While most of what we do as human beings is concerned with the *quality* of life, we must have a life to which to give quality. Were this not so we would hardly have spent so much of our time and other precious resources on problems like curing cancer.

German Critical Psychologists adopt a concept of emergent evolution, i.e. a view that recognizes the development of new and irreducible qualities, as the key to their synthesis. In working out their position they have formulated critiques of both ordinary, mainstream, empiricist psychology and the more 'humanistic' alternatives like phenomenology and hermeneutics. On the basis of these critiques they have laid the foundation for a new kind of psychology that is both scientific in a recognizable sense and humanistic at the same time. As we shall see, this has involved re-evaluation of everything from the most basic philosophical assumptions to procedures in research and practice.

In putting this account together, I have had to decide on a balance between straight exposition of the work of the German Critical Psychologists and criticisms that have been brought against it. Critical Psychology was born in criticism, and current representatives of the position do not assume for a moment that the process has ended in their work. It is self-consciously a *Grundlegung* (laying of a groundwork) and it is fully expected that further development will require a process of continuous, constructive criticism. Indeed, the German Critical Psychologists have been among their own most severe critics. In any case, since the present effort will be the first introductory account of the position in English, I have deliberately attempted to stress exposition over external criticism, although some of the latter may be introduced in appropriate places.

Psychology is not isolated from societal practice, nor is it simply a set of rules given once and for all to be learned by rote. Yet this is how it is all too frequently presented in our textbooks, seminars, and lecture halls. German Critical Psychology is a reminder to us that psychology is, as Francis Bacon described science in *The Great Instauration* of 1620, 'not an opinion to be held but a work to be done' (Warhaft 1965: 310). It is a quest, not just for knowledge itself but for knowledge that will serve human beings in their efforts to realize the quality of life made possible by their productive labours. Whatever else we may finally take from it this lesson should not be missed. It is a task we must make our own if psychology is to have any value for a genuine understanding of subjective human existence.

This book will not deal with everything the Critical Psychologists have done or said, nor with what has been said about their work by others. Indeed, it is doubtful that I have come anywhere near saying what, in any comprehensive account, needs to be said. In many respects the book will raise more questions than it answers. I feel on completing it, as I imagine Calvin Hall must have felt when he wrote his famous *A Primer of Freudian Psychology* (1955), that such a rich body of thought could not possibly be done justice in so few pages. Yet Hall's book and others like it provided an important first foothold for many of us. I only hope the present book, despite its necessary deficiencies, will do the same.

Finally, before beginning, the reader should be alerted to the fact that Critical Psychology was a product of the intellectual ferment associated with the student movement of the late 1960s. As such, it arises out of a highly charged political context and remains political in its own programme to the end. Political protest is not a gentle business. The book begins with the tragic death of a student protester, a galvanizing event that, as the reader will see, played a significant role in the development of Critical Psychology. If psychology is to be relevant to real life, it must begin with real life.

Charles W. Tolman
Victoria, British Columbia

Acknowledgements

There would be no critical psychology of the form described in this book had it not been for the genius of Klaus Holzkamp. He would insist that he was not alone in producing this psychology. There are important historical predecessors, and essential contributions have been made by a large number of other individuals. In writing this book I am indebted to all of them in one way or another. In particular, however, I have learned about critical psychology from my close association with Wolfgang Maiers. The work of Ute Osterkamp, Morus Markard, and Karl-Heinz Braun has also been particularly helpful to my understanding. Comments on the manuscript of this book by Wolfgang Maiers have spared me from embarrassing errors and misunderstandings. John Broughton and David Ingleby have made useful suggestions and saved me from some mortifyingly muddled prose.

I am grateful to Campus Verlag of Frankfurt, Germany, for their permission to cite extensive sections of Klaus Holzkamp's *Grundlegung der Psychologie* (1983) in translated form, and to Fischer Taschenbuch Verlag, also of Frankfurt, for their permission to cite and translate sections of Holzkamp's *Kritische Psychologie: Vorbereitende Arbeiten* (1972).

Work on this book, and much that led up to it, was supported by grants from the University of Victoria and from the Social Science and Humanities Research Council of Canada.

Closer to home, I have been fortunate to have had the constant and active support of my partner, Renate Eulig-Tolman. She has helped me, sometimes puzzled with me, through innumerable passages of difficult and otherwise impossible German text. She has patiently listened as I engaged in overt self-clarification. She has contributed substantively and significantly to that clarification by her own wisdom and erudition. She has been an unwavering source of support – moral, emotional, and every other kind. To say that this book could not have been written without her is to say far too little, but, as all who put pen to paper (or fingertip to keyboard) know, insufficiency is all too often the way of words.

Part I

Dissent

Chapter 1

Ideology, power, and subjectivity

Berlin, 2 July 1967, 8.20 p.m. The life of Benno Ohnesorg is ended by a bullet fired from a police pistol. Ohnesorg was 26 years old, married, a student of Germanic and Romance languages and literature at the Free University of Berlin. He did not have a reputation for being radical or even particularly political. His only active affiliation was with the Evangelical Congregation at the university.

The Shah of Iran was in Berlin on an official state visit. On 1 July there had been a meeting of about 2,000 students at the Free University to protest against the Shah's friendly reception by the city and federal governments. They heard testimony of the Shah's cruel and unjust treatment of his own people from an exiled Iranian. They were already acquainted with the circumstances of the Shah's restoration to power by the CIA, the same CIA now identified with the increasingly unpopular war in Vietnam. A decision was taken to demonstrate the following day as the Shah arrived at the city hall. There was also to be a protest in the evening outside the Opera House where the Shah and his wife, together with a gathering of carefully selected German dignitaries, were to attend a special performance.

The afternoon's demonstration started like most of the demonstrations that had become increasingly frequent in the preceding two years. It might have ended in the usual way too, but for one thing. The Shah had brought his own cheering team of about 80 men dressed in business suits and carrying clubs of about four feet in length. While the students were being kept at a distance from the city hall by barricades, these 'Shah boosters' ranged freely in the intervening space. At some point, in response to jeers, they let loose with their clubs on the student demonstrators. After a few moments of this, the police came on to the scene in force, not to restrain the Shah's henchmen but to assist them in dispersing the students.

News of this travesty spread quickly, with the result that in the evening at the Opera House the number of demonstrators was larger than expected and the mood decidedly more acrimonious. No attempt was made by police to keep protesters away from the scene, but the demonstrators, once there, were shoved by a force of about 800 policemen back on to the sidewalk across the wide avenue from the Opera House and squeezed between a wall at their backs and police barricades on the street side. The Shah and his party arrived. Placards were waved, slogans shouted, and chants sounded: 'Mo-Mo-Mossadegh!' 'Shah, Shah, Charlatan!' Just before 8 o'clock all the dignitaries had arrived and the doors of the Opera House were closed. The crowd of demonstrators was about to break up, some urging others to return at 10 o'clock, others discussing where to go for a beer and conversation. A few minutes later, the president of police, Erich Duening, apparently unhappy with the slowness with which the students were leaving, gave the order: 'Truncheons out, disperse the crowd!'

The police attacked. For most of the students there was nowhere to go. Those at either end of the confined crowd fled down the broad avenue, others took to adjoining side streets with police in pursuit. A few of these found themselves cornered in a covered parking area. Benno Ohnesorg was among them.

Someone reported hearing a young man's voice: 'Please, please, don't shoot.' There was a shot. A policeman was heard to say: 'You must be crazy, you could have hit one of us.' Frank Krüger, a music student, was an eye-witness:

> I was right there when the shot went off. I saw how a swarm of six or eight policemen attacked the student [Ohnesorg], how they went after him with their truncheons, how he just stood there in the midst of them, passive and defence-less. Then I saw the flash from the pistol. It was at about head level. In the next moment the student was lying on the ground, motionless.
>
> ('Knüppel frei' 1967: 46)

At first the police claimed that Ohnesorg died of a skull fracture. It was soon admitted, however, that it was a bullet in the head. The police officer Karl-Heinz Kurras, at the time in plain clothes, claimed he shot in self-defence. This claim was at first accepted by the police and Senate but a later inquiry showed it to be untenable and Kurras was charged with negligent homicide. The trial was held the following November. The court determined that Kurras had indeed pulled the trigger but it could not decide his actual culpability. On this technicality he was acquitted.

No matter what side is taken, all widely accepted accounts of the student movement in Germany agree that this incident represented the single most important, galvanizing moment in the movement's development, a development in which the Free University of Berlin played a leading role and which ultimately produced a critical psychology. In order to understand this we need to look backward from the Ohnesorg incident in order to see how the Free University of Berlin became the centre of political and academic dissidence in Germany, and forward from it to see how the killing's galvanizing effect expressed itself in the academic scene at the university.[1]

ORIGINS OF THE FREE UNIVERSITY OF BERLIN (FUB)

Berlin got its university in 1810, rather late by European standards. The driving force behind its establishment had been Wilhelm von Humboldt. It was named after the Prussian king Friedrich Wilhelm. Under his name it came to its end in 1945 after 12 years of Nazi rule. By the end of the war the university lay in both physical and moral ruins. Its principal physical location was on the avenue Unter den Linden, which was now in the Soviet sector of the divided city. The Soviet military administration set about its reconstruction almost immediately. Until 1948 the British and French occupation authorities displayed a total lack of interest in the university. The Americans were ambivalent. While they half-heartedly entertained ultimately un-fruitful plans for their own involvement in the re-establishment of higher education in Berlin, the military authorities took active measures to prevent students at the re-opened university from residing in the American sector and to prevent residents of their sector from attending the university.

The restarted university and its students suffered as well from ambivalences of a different sort. The Soviet authorities promised a free and democratic institu-tion that would put itself at the disposal of young people who, under more ordinary circumstances, would not have been able to attend university. This was primarily to affect people from the lower middle and working classes. Others who had suffered under the Nazis were also to be favoured. At first, the promise was largely kept and the students enthusiastically embraced the new freedom. Interference from the authorities increased, however, reaching a peak in March 1947 when several student leaders were arrested for allegedly spying for the West. This was only one sign of the mounting Cold War. The year that followed saw an increased tightening of control with politically motivated demotions of faculty and dismissals of students. Finally, after the dismissal of some key student political leaders, a strike was called for 23 April 1948 and students were urged to attend a meeting at the Hotel Esplanade in the British sector. The Eastern press reported that only 300 students showed up. Western papers reported 2,000. This meeting played a key role in motivating the Americans to establish an alternative university in their sector.

From the very start, there was widespread suspicion of the Americans' motives, certainly in the East but also in the West. Whatever the motives, however, a new university was founded in 1948 with a large contribution of funds from the Ford Foundation. Basically, the new university presented itself as undertaking to deliver on the promises about freedom and democracy with which the old one, now called the Humboldt University, had been re-opened. Much to their credit, the Americans left most of the university's organization to the Germans, including students, many of whom had migrated over from the 'Linden University', bringing with them many of the progressive ideals that had been disappointed there. They continued, for instance, to insist on a significant student voice in administration and preferential admission for members of disadvantaged groups. The end result was unique in the history of German universities. The new Free University of Berlin represented a progressive model that would continue to attract politically concerned students from all parts of Germany over the decades that followed. The Free University of Berlin, in short, had its beginning in protest and dissidence, and soon established a tradition of anti-elitist, anti-authoritarian, politically tolerant and progressive thought and practice.[2]

BEGINNINGS OF THE STUDENT MOVEMENT

The tradition of political engagement established at the Free University could hardly remain confined, however, to the precincts of the university itself. The university was, after all, quite self-consciously an aspect of the society around it. It could also not continue to develop without straining its limits. It seems now in retrospect that political engagement would necessarily turn into protest and finally spill over on to the streets of the city itself. One of the first public demonstrations occurred in December 1964, when several hundred students protested at the visit of Moïse Tshombé, the premier of the Congo, whom they held responsible for the death of the popular leftist leader Patrice Lumumba.

A turning point in this connection was reached in the spring of 1965. The student government, AStA (*Allgemeiner Studenten-Ausschuss*), invited a journalist and two other guests to take part in a symposium or debate on the political course taken by Germany since the war. The journalist, Erich Kuby, had been critical of the FUB administration since 1949 and had already been declared *persona non grata* in 1958 by the Rector, who then refused to allow Kuby to speak at the university on two occasions in 1960 and 1963. Rector Herbert Lüers once again intervened, refusing to allow Kuby to speak. The students, doubtless taking their cue from the 'Free Speech Movement' at the University of California, protested that their rights under the university's constitution were being violated. They claimed the right to hear any person speak in any open area on campus at any time on any subject. A series of strikes and demonstrations ensued involving over 3,000 students. This set of events marked the beginning in earnest of the student protest movement at the FUB. The number and frequency of public demonstrations increased after May 1965. The issues ranged widely from local ones concerning the administration of the university to international ones, becoming increasingly focused on the Vietnam war. In April 1967 a group of students was arrested for allegedly plotting against the life of the American vice-president, Hubert Humphrey. Police searches, however, only turned up some small smoke-bombs and a large supply of powdered pudding mix. The students called themselves the 'Horror Commune', but they became better known as the 'pudding assassins'. Whatever humour may have been expressed in the idea of slinging pudding at an American vice-president vanished with the death of Benno Ohnesorg.[3]

THE 'CRITICAL UNIVERSITY'

The seriousness of protest not only increased in intensity, it also increased in scope. Criticism, initially focused on violations of rights within the university, had generalized to criticism of city, state, national, and international policy now finally to knowledge itself, its production, dissemination, and relation to practice. With regard to the dissemination of knowledge, for instance, Axel Springer, owner of several popular right-leaning newspapers and magazines in Germany (not to be confused with the highly reputable Springer Verlag), became a particular target of the FUB student movement under the leadership of Rudi Dutschke. Dutschke cited Springer for gross misuse of his ideological power and called for the expropriation of his publishing empire ('Wir fordern' 1967). But the most important single event for our concern here was the founding in July 1967 of the Critical University.[4]

The Critical University was organized by Wolfgang Lefèvre, president of the FUB student assembly, Sigrid Fronius, and Wolfgang Nitsch from the Max-Planck-Institute for Educational Research, with the cooperation of about 40 other students and faculty members. Their critique began with their own institutions. According to their 'calendar' (of which 6,000 copies were printed), the old-style institutions of higher learning, including now the FUB, 'had finally transformed themselves from ivory towers into ivory factories in which professorial specialty-idiots trained student specialty-idiots' ('Dr. crit.' 1967). They urged that henceforth the students forming the elite left would have to lead double lives: half idiot and half revolutionary. It was the function of the Critical University to look after the revolutionary side.

The self-defined tasks of the Critical University, now divided among 30 working groups, were double in nature. On the one hand, they were to attempt to form alliances with workers. They would offer educational workshops for working people and assist them in diagnosing the problems they faced in a bourgeois-dominated society and in formulating effective political action. On the other hand, they would conduct critical activity within the FUB, holding seminars on the political aspects of education, criticizing course contents, examinations, and the educational aims and practices of German universities in general.

Needless to say, the administrative authorities of the FUB denied the Critical University use of any of its facilities and even undertook a legal examination of its programme and activities to determine if charges might be brought against the students involved. The Critical University managed, however, to survive long enough to fuel further developments of a similar nature.

A leaflet circulating at the University of Mainz read:

In Berlin people are now being shot, but not just at the wall. In East Berlin demonstrations are prohibited; in West Berlin demonstrations are prohibited. In East Berlin what the Magistrate doesn't like is suppressed; in West Berlin what the Senate doesn't like is suppressed. Berlin remains Berlin.

('Knüppel frei' 1967: 46)

DEVELOPMENTS IN THE PSYCHOLOGICAL INSTITUTE

Meanwhile, in the Psychological Institute debates were taking on a more openly political nature. One in particular was to set the tone for what was to follow. Professor Hans Hörmann, then director of the Institute, had reiterated his 'liberal' view of the relation between psychology and society as part of his address at a memorial service at the FUB for Benno Ohnesorg. Hörmann's understanding of this relationship put the individual conscience at the centre. Psychology as science was accordingly essentially value-free. Psychology's link to values and societal practice was the individual psychologist. It was up to the individual to see that psychological knowledge was used in the correct interests. Judgement of correctness was also left up to the individual. This was a judgement, in Hörmann's view, that no individual could escape.

An impassioned and eloquent rebuttal based theoretically on the Critical Theory of Theodor Adorno and Jürgen Habermas[5] came from a student of the Institute, Irmingard Staeuble. Hörmann's view, she maintained, showed insufficient appreciation for the essentially political nature of science. It was just such an innocuous view of science that had encouraged the conclusion – false, in her view – that the universities during the Third Reich had merely been used by the Nazis and that the proper corrective had been to return universities to their more 'natural' state of neutrality, leaving implications for the well-being of society to the responsibility of the individual conscience. By Staeuble's analysis, science and the universities were never neutral; they existed necessarily in one interest or another. Fact and consciousness were always mediated by societal and historical context. The boundaries between philosophy, science, ideology, and society faded under this analysis, revealing a necessary, interrelated whole. Psychologists who failed to see this were simply putting themselves blindly into the service of prevailing ideologies.

A little later, Staeuble offered these biting observations on contemporary psychology:

> Looking at the areas in which psychologists have mainly been active, it must be concluded that (a) they work in the immediate service of imperialism (military research, 'psychological defence'); (b) they work in the service of the capitalist economy (market research, advertising); (c) they have an indirect effect on the stabilization of bourgeois ideology (research on communications and opinion); (d) they advance the efficient performance of individuals within the system of this society (selection methods of all kinds, industrial psychology, occupational counselling); and (e) they are contributing to social conformity (all sorts of counselling).
>
> (Staeuble 1968, quoted in Holzkamp 1972: 217)[6]

The basis of the critique would eventually move away from Habermasian Critical Theory but the essential conclusion would remain the same: psychology is an unavoidably political endeavour.

THE 'EMERGENCY LAW' OF 1968

1968 saw another student shot. This time the target was the charismatic student leader, Rudi Dutschke, and the would-be assassin was not a policeman but a disturbed young man, apparently fired up by the hysterical rhetoric of the popular press. Dutschke survived only to die of complications from his injuries in 1979.

The year also saw the introduction of an Emergency Law that would effectively curb any freedom of speech that still remained for the dissident students.[7]

As already noted above, some politicization had been taking place in the Psychological Institute well before 1968, most of it focused, as implied in Staeuble's remarks, on the critique of positivist notions of science. It was the Emergency Law, however, that precipitated the major changes that would come to shape and characterize the study of psychology at the FUB. According to Klaus Holzkamp, referring mainly to the debate between Hörmann and Staeuble:

[T]he first controversy arose among some students [in the Institute] about the politicization of the university. This led to two further organized discussions but had little noticeable effect. Only on the occasion of the campaign against the Emergency Law in the spring of 1968 did a large majority of students and assistants in the Institute decide for political action. For 14 days all lectures and seminars were devoted to discussion of the Emergency Law. A vigorous programme of disseminating information and other forms of political action was undertaken. From that time forward the work of the Institute assumed a new quality: discussions about democratic reform of the Institute were launched by the newly formed 'ad hoc group' of progressive students. The Psychological Institute was unique among the institutes of the University in that faculty members joined the students in initiating and supporting the work of reform. During the summer break of 1968 various of the Institute's functions, from research planning to admissions and budget, were scrutinized by ten committees, and the results were reported in detail to the Institute at large.

(Holzkamp 1972: 212)

THE 'CONGRESS OF CRITICAL AND OPPOSITIONAL PSYCHOLOGY'

In September 1968 the congress of the German Society for Psychology was held at Tübingen. A symposium on psychology and political behaviour had just got under way when the room was invaded by a group of about 20 students, mainly from the Technical University of Berlin, an institution separate from the FUB. The spokesman for the group took the podium and announced that they had 'heard enough theses, had been frustrated long enough', and it was now time for them to put forward their 'own theses'. There were 27 of these, criticizing every imaginable aspect of current psychological research, teaching, and practice. A discussion followed, focusing mainly on alleged political misuses of psychology:

Psychological research is supposed to be important for society, but who decides what is important? Is restriction of the freedom of research by social control acceptable? And, anyway, who is doing the controlling? Are individual scientists responsible for the misuse of their research findings? How can those with no power in society prevent such misuse?

(Holzkamp 1972: 220)

The criticisms were listed and questions asked, but no firm answers were forth-
coming on that occasion.

This led to an important event in May 1969: the Congress of Critical and
Oppositional Psychology, held in Hannover and attended by students and psychologists from all over the Federal Republic. The intention was to resolve the
questions raised the previous fall in Tübingen. After two days of discussion,
students from the Technical University of Berlin (TU) presented a resolution
summarizing their own conclusions. They had become pessimistic about the
whole affair. Three basic tendencies, they said, could be identified in the discussion of the preceding two days: (1) 'critical enlightenment', that is, a lot of
high-flown liberal verbiage with little connection to real praxis; (2) 'petty bourgeois terror', which amounted to advocating 'orgiastic' actions aimed at the
mindless venting of frustration; and (3) 'reformist fiddling' that might patch up a
thing or two, but would leave things essentially unchanged. In short, all solutions
that sought to remain *psychological* remained effectively *unpolitical*. Political
solutions, they maintained, were not psychological. The reason for this was that
psychology 'has been and always will be an instrument of those in power'. They
were thus led to the following practical recommendations:

1. Make existing psychological knowledge – as knowledge of the system –
   part of the struggle against the system! (For example, put an end to the use
   of intelligence tests as instruments of domination by publicly distributing
   copies and analyses of them.)
2. Subvert psychology in the institutes!
3. Develop an offensive strategy wherever psychology is used in the evaluation process!
   There is no 'critical' or 'oppositional' psychology! That means there is
   no revolutionary psychology! SMASH PSYCHOLOGY!

(Holzkamp 1972: 222)

The delegation from the FUB was of a different mind, and on the following day they
presented a formal reply to various charges made by the TU group. First, they
maintained that the possibility of a progressive, politically engaged, critical psychology had not had a fair hearing during the first two days precisely because those who
now wanted to abandon the project had themselves obstructed discussion. Second,
the TU group had defined real political praxis as only that which was not integrated
into capitalism. Since it is hard to see how anything could not be integrated into
capitalism, this would reduce the possibilities for real political action to zero.

The third point of the FUB response objected to the claim that the only
alternative was to 'smash psychology' just because it is a necessary instrument of
those in power. They noted the apparent irony of smashing psychology as a
concrete alternative, and offered a somewhat different analysis:

We agree that it is not possible to use the dominant psychology – precisely
because it is the psychology of those in power – to produce an analysis of the

present state of society. For this, questions must be asked that bourgeois psychology does not ask. These are the questions that result directly from the need for revolutionary change of society, and only answers to these questions will make an adequate analysis of the present system possible. This does not imply falling into the bourgeois error of expecting to change conditions by psychological means alone. . . . We think that critical psychology (that is, psychology within the sphere of Critical Theory), within a framework of revolutionary strategy, can achieve not only instrumental but also cognitive value, such as clarifying what constitutes a concrete liberated existence and by informing us about the psychological processes that mediate domination. Even bourgeois psychology is not, as alleged, confined to description. It seeks to analyse conditions, although it is limited in this by its bourgeois ideology (as, for example, in the case of sexuality) and, under the assumption of value-neutrality, supports domination.

(Holzkamp 1972: 223)

They offered the following analysis of psychology as it was taught and practised in the institutes:

1 As *description* it portrayed mediated categories as unmediated (as in the nativistic conception of aggression), thus hypostatizing and ontologizing the status quo.
2 As an *analysis of conditions* it excluded non-psychological categories, re-stricting itself to psychological contexts, thus depoliticizing itself within the scientific division of labour.
3 As *prognosis* it served technical evaluation and control, thus suspending the self-determination of individuals in favour of determination by others.
4 It *abstained from value judgements*, rationalizing itself as value-neutral and ignoring societal reality; it remained in an ivory tower, accumulating trivialities and repressing its own effect on the lives of people.

A contrasting *critical psychology* could be defined as no mere reflex-reaction to the dominant logical-empirical psychology but as an integral part of the social sciences aimed at the possibility of a human existence liberated from oppression and misery in accordance with the emancipatory claims of Critical Theory (Holzkamp 1972: 223–224).

One need not, in short, throw the baby out with the bath water. If psychology as currently practised is biased in favour of those who hold power, a critical psychology, one that would be biased in favour of the powerless, cannot be ruled out. This formed the outline of the basic programme that the FUB group would attempt to articulate and develop in the years that followed.

DEMOCRATIZATION OF THE PSYCHOLOGICAL INSTITUTE

In the mean time the students and faculty of the Psychological Institute at the FUB undertook a radical democratization of the Institute based largely on the work done by the ten committees during the summer break of 1968. The final result of this work, which was completed at the end of January 1969, was a total restructuring of the Institute's administrative and decision-making organization. According to the new plan the Institute would no longer be run by an *Ordinarius* (full professor) acting in the capacity of Director. Rather, it would be run by an Institute Council made up of representatives from all concerned groups including students, secretarial and technical staff, and junior and senior faculty. The new statutes of the Institute announced:

> The Institute Council advises and decides when it finds it necessary on all questions concerning the Institute, which it for itself determines to be import-ant or that are brought forward by members or groups in the Institute as defined by these statutes. . . . The administrative officers of the Institute are obliged . . . to carry out the decisions of the Institute Council.
>
> (Holzkamp 1972: 234)

This change in the Institute was greeted at the time as marking the beginning of a new democratic epoch, and would have a number of repercussions that signifi-cantly influenced the further development of Critical Psychology. One of these came as a jolt to the more idealistic participants in the new democratization. For some the new freedom was taken to mean freedom from anything resembling the authoritarian state and a manipulative society; it meant the 'great refusal'. The new statutes invited this: within an oppressive institution, revolutionary struggle had produced a 'free space', a space in which the individual was free to refuse the dictates of any authority and what might be taken as manipulation by others. The emphasis appeared to have moved from the revolutionary emancipation of *society* to emancipation of *the individual within bourgeois society*. This under-standing found support in both Critical Theory and in psychoanalysis in both its 'classical' and 'sex-pol' versions.[8] The unity of personal life-style and political activity could be achieved by resisting the pressures of an achievement-oriented society. In the work of the Institute this was translated into the refusal to achieve or to conform academically or in any other way. Students urged the abandonment of examinations and the right to sign their own certificates of performance. Absence from and late arrivals to lectures and seminars became commonplace. If and when they were used, seminar rooms and lecture halls were left in a deplor-ably untidy condition.

Klaus Holzkamp later summarized the lesson learnt from this:

> Sensitivity to the suffering inflicted on people by this society had reached such heights that a struggle against such suffering became unavoidable. But it was not yet understood that from this suffering, as social suffering, there could be no individual alleviation, that the idea of a repressionless 'free space' within bourgeois society *is itself a bourgeois, idealistic notion*. Nevertheless, it would be wrong and ahistorical simply to dismiss the struggle for personal and political free space. The insight, gained less from intellectual reflection than

from painful experience, that 'freedom' in this society cannot mean individual liberation from the demands of society and related suffering was an important step in the development of the political consciousness of the left. Socialists at the university learned that freedom for the individual could only mean insight into the necessity for a long-term, privation-filled, disciplined programme of work towards the goal of scientific socialism.

(Holzkamp 1972: 236)

At the first meeting of the new Institute Council the need felt by students to engage in revolutionary practice produced a proposal for an after-school programme for underprivileged children in Kreuzberg, a working-class district of Berlin with a high proportion of immigrant workers. The programme would be called 'Red Freedom' and was intended to involve students in a kind of anti-authoritarian, political consciousness-raising among school children. The formal proposal failed to identify clearly its theoretical justification and had many other defects as well, but senior members of the council saw it as a test of their newly proclaimed confidence in the students and feared that refusal, or even insistence on its being better thought through, would be construed in authoritarian terms and evoke further student resistance. On the more positive side there was a distinct possibility that theoretical understanding would develop through self-assessment of the action. Klaus Holzkamp agreed to join the collective and share responsibility for the project. As he said later, 'isolation of the students was to be avoided at all costs, because the development of a programme of progressive teaching and research could only be achieved through the gradual reorganization of the *entire Institute*' (Holzkamp 1972: 239). Among those in the Institute who could not accept such a decision was the director, Professor Hans Hörmann. He took the opportunity presented by an offer from the University of Bochum to leave Berlin.

THE NEW UNIVERSITY LAW OF 1969 AND THE RED CELL MOVEMENT

Important changes came with a new University Law in August 1969. The law was intended to do two things. First, it would restructure the university to make it more 'manageable'. This was to be accomplished through the abolition of the old faculties and the establishment in their place of new administrative disciplinary groupings called *Fachbereiche* (divisions). Second, it would respond to the demands of the students and junior faculty for a greater say in the affairs of the university. The decision-making bodies were to consist of full professors, mid-level faculty,[9] and students. Their relative contributions to the process, however, were not to be equal. Votes were to be weighted in the ratio 7:4:3. On the grounds that students would have their voices adequately expressed in this fashion the traditional student governing body, AStA, was officially abolished.

The administrative restructuring required a period of discussion aimed at deciding what divisions would be formed and from what disciplines they were to be constituted. A majority of the Psychological Institute's council favoured a Division of Philosophy and Social Sciences which would include philosophy, psychology, sociology, and journalism. A minority favoured the inclusion of education. In the end, the debate within and among the disciplines came down in favour of the Institute Council's majority position.

The student response to the abolition of AStA in favour of being made a part of the official decision-making structure was found unacceptable by a large proportion of the students, particularly those who identified themselves as left. They saw the restructuring as a blatant cooptation and demanded an independent body. Failing to get this officially, they organized their own, which became known as the 'Red Cell' movement. Red Cells were organized to parallel the new university structure. Red Cell councils were thus established for each institute and division.

The founding of the Red Cell council in the Psychological Institute had two rather different consequences. Most immediately, it exacerbated the tensions that had been developing between the left and liberal elements in the Institute. The Left held a slight majority in the Institute Council and appeared determined to use it to advance their own programmes. The Liberals, although initially supportive of the democratic restructuring of the Institute, came to feel increasingly alienated. Tensions came to a head in early 1970 when a committee of the Division of Philosophy and Social Sciences made its recommendation that the position vacated the previous year by Professor Hörmann be filled by Professor Klaus Eyferth. Unfortunately, the student representatives on this committee had failed to use their right to consult with the students at large, and thus for them the announcement came as a surprise. Protests were immediately made and briefs against the appointment of Eyferth were prepared by both students and mid-level faculty, who invited Eyferth to decline the appointment. After lengthy discussions with all concerned and several months of deliberation Eyferth did decline.

This was an unfortunate event at that particular time for several reasons. First, the appointment itself was badly managed. It was made to appear authoritarian just when everyone was ultrasensitive to appearances of authoritarianism and every measure was being taken to avoid it. It was also unfortunate because the actions it evoked, culminating in Eyferth's declining to accept the appointment, provided the impetus for two further calamitous events. The first was a demand by the liberal minority in the Institute that they be reconstituted as a separate institute in the Division of Education. This was resisted by the left majority but finally approved and effected. The second event was the beginning of a public campaign in the newspapers against the Psychological Institute. It is not hard to imagine what a conservative press would make of the combination of events: the after-school programme 'Red Freedom'; the growing influence in the Institute of its Red Cell; the interference with the legal appointment of a new professor on what appeared to be political grounds; and the disaffection to the point of secession of the liberal students and faculty.

Leadership of the campaign against the Left generally was taken up by the Berlin Senator for the Sciences and Arts. A series of lectures by three Marxist scholars entitled 'Literature on the Restoration of Capital in West Germany' was scheduled for the winter semester 1970/71 by the Red Cell in the Institute for Germanic Studies. The Senator declared these lectures to be inimical to the Constitution (*verfassungswidrig*) and ordered them to be cancelled. Not just the students and faculty but also the President of the FU resisted this blatant interference by state authority. The University took the matter officially to the Administrative Court of Berlin, which, on 12 January 1971, declared in favour of the University. The Senator's ban was lifted and the lectures went ahead. Ironically, the court declared not the lectures but the Senator's interference to be inimical to the Constitution.

The campaign against the Psychological Institute, however, did not end so easily, fairly, or quickly. Needless to say, most of the publicity was extremely one-sided and sensationalistic. One of the nastier aspects of the campaign was the way in which it came to focus on the person of Klaus Holzkamp because of his involvement with the 'Red Freedom' collective. He soon found attempts at explanation and justification to be useless. 'That it was a scandal had already been decided' (Holzkamp 1972: 251). Again, a lesson was learned from the experience:

> I had to learn that these public attacks on me could not be taken personally. Either such attacks are, as they were here, incidentally provoked, in which case they came to be taken as the occasion to learn more about the mechanisms by which such public reactions originate. Or we simply conclude that such public attacks cannot be avoided in some kinds of scientific-political activity; they just have to be accepted as part of the everyday task.
>
> (Holzkamp 1972: 250)

THE TURN TO MARXISM

The advent of the Red Cells had a more positive consequence. Their members in the Psychological Institute, as elsewhere in the FUB, had been part of the 'Marx renaissance' of the late 1960s. Unlike many of the other radical activists of the student movement, they had a clearer idea of their goals in terms of socialism and a better appreciation of the effects of their actions. They also knew that effective action required real theoretical knowledge and the persistence of long-term programmes. These qualities were already evident in the founding document of the Red Cell of the Psychological Institute, dated 11 March 1969:

> The actual socialist praxis of the various projects having to do with socialization and the theoretical working groups associated with them needs a political organization that sets out obligatory perspectives that are goal-directed and long term. . . . Agitation represents the attempt to find political insights in the context of societal domination, which seek to break through the character of the elitist accumulation of knowledge so as to initiate a broader

solidarity. Optimal agitation requires a political education in which theoretical knowledge and development of political consciousness form a part of the overall revolutionary strategy. Socialist praxis is conditional upon a political consciousness among its participants that recognizes the concrete necessities and possibilities of revolutionary change in late capitalism. It must be understood as an initiation into the revolutionizing process of the wage-earning masses, through whose consciousness alone the actual inversion of all societal relations can be achieved. . . . The work of the organization takes place in three areas: education, agitation, and praxis. These are constituting moments of one and the same process, and may not be separated.

(Holzkamp 1972: 241–242)

The Red Cells organized study groups on a variety of topics from educational reform to scientific methods. Most prominent, however, was the study of dialectical and historical materialism, for which Marx's *Introduction to the Critique of Political Economy* and *Capital* provided the main texts. In the Psychological Institute an officially recognized course on the 'Critique of Political Economy' was offered during the winter semester of 1969.

Their emphasis on the necessity of theoretical work caused tensions with the activists associated with Red Freedom, who regarded their Red Cell counterparts as 'seminar Marxists'. This friction initiated an important debate on the relationship between theory and practice, which proved generally beneficial to both sides by providing an opportunity to resolve some basic questions through study and self-criticism. The relationship between the two groups remained relatively nonantagonistic. In any event, they consistently managed to form a solid front against the liberals on questions relating to the Institute, especially the appointment of Professor Eyferth. This solidarity contributed substantially to the establishment by the liberals of a separate institute.

KLAUS HOLZKAMP AND CRITICAL PSYCHOLOGY

Prior to 1970, Klaus Holzkamp had published two important books on method in psychology (1964, 1968). In these works he had developed a critique of logical empiricist methods and knowledge claims within a framework that became known as 'constructivist'. During 1970 and 1972, he published a series of articles on methodology and psychological knowledge, each becoming increasingly critical of his own earlier 'constructivist' work. They also reflected the influence of the events in the Psychological Institute and the FUB that we have described. This was not only the case with respect to the kinds of problems addressed, such as the relevance of psychological knowledge, but also in basic metatheoretical orientation. Most notable was the shift to a clear Marxist position by 1972. These articles were collected and the transition critically discussed in a book published in 1972, *Kritische Psychologie: Vorbereitende Arbeiten* (*Critical Psychology: Preparatory Works*). The general programme of Holzkamp's Critical Psychology[10] was not entirely transparent in this book. It did express, however, the principal concerns that would motivate the development of that programme over the succeeding years. A concern that was pivotal was that of relevance.

The relevance of prescribed studies has been an early concern of the student movement in Berlin as elsewhere. The problem arose, in part, because there existed a relationship, even if not always clear, between relevance and value. Although there appeared to be an inherent connection between what is valued and what is considered relevant, the traditional empiricist view of knowledge, particularly of scientific knowledge, portrayed it as essentially value-free. It seemed, then, to follow that knowledge could not be inherently relevant. To the extent that value or relevance was an issue, then, it was one of individual judgement. This was the position expressed by Professor Hörmann at the memorial service for Benno Ohnesorg. It may seem to be a move in the right direction to go beyond the individual interest to societal interests. As Irmingard Staeuble noted in her response to Hörmann, however, this alone does not resolve the problem. What is to say why the interests of one group like the Nazis should or should not prevail over those of others? One is still faced with an unresolvable relativity. It has simply been shifted to a broader scale.

This problem was also central to the initial reaction of many students to the democratization of the Psychological Institute. Democratization, that is, giving the individual a greater say over his or her personal fate in a society or in an institution, is aimed at making the experience more relevant. It soon became evident, however, that if relevance was to be interpreted in so personal a fashion, the institution, and indeed society, could be brought to a virtual standstill in which no one would benefit. The history of the Psychological Institute confirmed, too, that the move from individual to group was not the solution.

FOCUSING ON THE CENTRAL QUESTIONS

Two issues were at stake here: relevance and the relationship between individual and society. There appeared to be a necessity in the latter of which the former was an aspect, which is why the group-interest solution appeared at first blush to have some promise. That solution proved to be flawed, however, suggesting that it had not been correctly formulated. As Irmingard Staeuble remarked in her 1968 presentation: 'Theory must measure up to something. However, since the thing . . . is not neutral but structured by society, theory cannot do without an adequate conception of society' (quoted in Holzkamp 1972: 216).[11] Relevance, it would seem, was already contained in the object of societal attention when science, that is, the scientist, came to it. The relevance of knowledge, from this point of view, was effectively equivalent to the adequacy of that knowledge. As Holzkamp put it later (1972: 284): '[I]n bourgeois society the substantive knowledge of social science is so to speak internally related – though in complex ways – to the degree and kind of its societal relevance.' The 'complex ways' imply the theory of society that Staeuble mentioned.

This, however, left an important problem unresolved. The question of personal relevance could not simply be bypassed by claiming that relevance was a societal issue. That was simply not the case: *personal* relevance still existed. It had been, after all, a widely held concern for personal relevance that had initiated the discussion. What was missing here was another aspect of the theory of society: that having to do with its relation to the individual.

When we turn to psychology we find no solution. The laws it offers are essentially ahistorical and asocietal. This is particularly apparent in the various forms of behaviourism. Behaviourists take pride in the generality of their laws of reinforcement. These laws tend, in fact, to be so general that differences between species, from invertebrates to humans, are totally obliterated (cf. Skinner 1956). This should not be a cause for scientific boasting but, on the contrary, one of grave concern. What is relevant to most of us is not how we are like pigeons but how we differ from them. The laws of schedules of reinforcement obviously are able to tell us nothing about what makes us specifically human. Indeed, they tell us little about animals of any kind. In opting for abstract generality over specificity, the behaviourist has had to abstract individual subjects from their phylogenetic and in the case of humans from their historical and societal natures.

One might object that this is only the case for extreme behaviourism. But this is not so. We can run the gamut of all the so-called alternative psychologies, from eclectic, through cognitive, to psychoanalytic and humanistic. We find the same problem: the isolation of individual subjects from their historical and societal contexts. When society is brought into the picture, as indeed it often is, it is done so as an external influence or variable that sets the abstracted, isolated individuals of our theories off against society and history as things external to them.

Not surprisingly, when we turn to sociology we find the problem not solved but simply inverted. In short, there is no theory in mainstream social science that effectively addresses the problem of the societal nature of the individual human subject. The end result is that the human subject is either totally subjectified or totally objectified, becoming abstracted and isolated in either case.

Yet this problem of the societal nature of the individual subject, that is, the relation of subjectivity to society, is frequently found at the heart of our most urgent concerns. The student movement was motivated by such a concern. All political struggles for democracy, for socialism, for a more humane society are reflections of a deep-seated need to better understand and deal with subjectivity in society.

The fact that over a century of intensive and extensive development of the mainstream social sciences by multitudes of highly intelligent and good-willed people has failed not only to solve this problem but even to address it in any broadly organized way leads us to at least two suppositions. On the one hand, we have to imagine that such a colossal failure must reflect some fundamental errors in our basic assumptions and methodologies. This would mean that, in order to make the needed correction, a profoundly radical assessment and reconstruction will be necessary. On the other hand, it suggests that the failure has not been entirely accidental but reflects the bias of a societal dynamic that itself must be understood. The needed radical critique must therefore be self-consciously both scientific-methodological and historical-ideological. What is needed found expression already in the Hörmann–Staeuble debate: a critique and reconstruction that brings us to a psychology that is *in itself critical*, not a psychology that may be made critical by the personal inclinations of the psychologist. It is such a critique and reconstruction that German Critical Psychology undertook and that I shall attempt to describe in the following chapters.

Part II

Critique

Chapter 2

Philosophical assumptions

Psychologists generally proceed with their work without stopping to reflect on the basic assumptions that underlie what they are doing. As students we learn how to do psychology. We learn about measurement, about validity and reliability, and about how to analyse relations among variables so as to arrive at general statements that can be accepted as psychological knowledge. We come to believe that to proceed in this way is to conform to the demands of science. All this requires us to make certain assumptions about the objects of our investigative procedures, about the nature of knowledge, and about the ways our methods link the two. The kind of science we thus produce is predetermined by its underlying assumptions, and such a science cannot, in principle, yield any data or other information that will disconfirm those assumptions. If there are fundamental flaws in our science, as Klaus Holzkamp and his colleagues came to suspect there were, it becomes essential to reflect on the assumptive framework itself. It is the effort by the Berlin Critical Psychologists to do this that I want to summarize in this chapter.

We already have good reason to believe that our science's philosophical assumptions are no less value-free than our psychological theories. If the latter reflect the values and priorities that govern the societal relations in which we work, it seems to follow necessarily for the former as well. It is in this connection that Critical Psychologists, in agreement with other critics of the current social order, Marxist and non-Marxist alike, speak of philosophy and scientific theory as 'bourgeois'. If we are agreed that neither philosophy nor science can be value-free, it makes good sense to identify modes of thought in terms of the values they represent. The society we live in is one characterized by a capitalist mode of production and those who wield power are either capitalists or people who have the interests of capitalism at heart. The historical rise of capitalism was at the same time the rise of a middle class known as the 'bourgeoisie'. The nature of capitalism and its dominant class has changed enormously since the days of the early mercantilists but the general designation remains appropriate. We can expect then that the prevailing social scientific theories and their underlying philosophies will reflect bourgeois values. A good part of *critical* theory is aimed precisely at exposing this fact and, where necessary, proposing alternatives that reflect new values.

It has been suggested by many people that in the present political climate it is bad tactics to speak of theories and philosophies as bourgeois. The intention here may be a good one but what are the alternatives? Frequently suggested are 'traditional' and 'mainstream'. The first suffers from indefiniteness: what tradition? This must, at some point, bring us back to 'bourgeois' since that is the tradition we are talking about. The second can lead us into a kind of obfuscation in which we lose the important distinction between unquestionably bourgeois theories that are mainstream and those that are definitely not. Humanistic psychology and, in the North American academy, psychoanalysis are cases in point. Both are bourgeois but neither is mainstream. In the end, avoiding the label 'bourgeois' encourages denial of or timidity about the very point we are trying to make: psychology *is* a political, societal practice and our task is to make this clear and overt in our thinking, our practice, and our language.

In taking a critical approach to bourgeois philosophy and theory, we want to be clear that the intention is not simply to 'smash' the old and replace it with its opposite. Critique is not a matter of simply condemning the dominant modes of thought. More constructively, it is aimed at exposing their 'one-sidedness'. For example, the socialist critique of bourgeois society is not aimed at 'smashing' the democracy and liberties that came to distinguish bourgeois society from the feudalism it replaced. The point is to show that, given the evolved societal productive capacity, bourgeois understandings of democracy and liberty are one-sided and abstract, and can only be made complete and concrete by their extension from the purely political sphere (e.g. the right to vote) to the economic sphere (e.g. the right to socially useful employment): what good does it do me if I can vote but have no guarantee of meaningful participation in the societal processes that assure the satisfaction of individual needs?

Likewise, we can expect that social scientific theories and the philosophies that support them have existed because they have served us in some important and useful way. What is right about them needs to be preserved in our critique. The heart of the issue is to recognize that the problem is an *historical* one: the theories and philosophies that are holding us back today were at one time themselves 'revolutionary' and 'progressive'. For example, the 'mechanicism' of science that is almost universally deplored today (though often silently maintained) played a significant historical role in providing people with greater control over their material lives and in breaking the ideological hold of feudal authority. The aim of a critical philosophy or science is to see that the historical process does not become bogged down but keeps pace with the expanded possibilities created by historical practice.

NAIVE EMPIRICISM

By far the most common philosophy of science forming the basis of general experimental psychology in this century has been the naive, common-sense, empiricism inherited from John Locke through nineteenth-century figures such as John Stuart Mill.[1] According to this position empirical science is concerned with the acquisition of true knowledge about nature. This knowledge is based on observation and experiment. From the data that these methods produce, generalizations are made by induction and, in favourable cases, may count as the discovery of natural law. Laws are considered as expressing something given in nature. Researchers are presumed to be searching for laws and the lucky ones find them. Research work is guided mainly by unbiased experience. In order to guarantee lack of bias, so that nature can, as it were, speak for itself, much of the researcher's activity is aimed at insuring his or her own passivity. The common metaphors of 'peering into the workshop of nature' and 'ferreting out nature's secrets' are reflections of naive empiricism.[2]

Holzkamp does not criticize this position for its emphasis on careful observation or for its expectations of true knowledge. Rather, his criticism is that naive empiricism allows no room for reflection on the question of relevance. Nature is understood as an ontologically given, pre-existing, ordered cosmos of laws, the scientist's task being to gain a foothold on some small piece of it, and then to proceed through further observation and experiment towards an increasingly comprehensive account of the independently given natural laws. It all depends on applying methods that are objective in the sense of excluding subjective judgement. If proper rules of method are followed, *there can be no substantively irrelevant scientific questions*. Any bit of new information at all, no matter how inconspicuous, is a stone in the mosaic and has a valid place in the lawful structure of nature. It therefore necessarily, however minimally, contributes to the enrichment of our true knowledge. Questions about the interests served by research have a simple answer. There is only one legitimate interest in scientific research and that is the acquisition of knowledge about nature. Scientists have their object, nature, which they confront with an attitude of objective curiosity. If scientific research is undertaken for any other than scientific reasons, such as political ones, its results will be invalidated by extra-scientific influences and will not be taken seriously by the scientific community.

Even earlier in this century, the *naïveté* of this position seemed to many so obvious that its mere description rendered a serious critique unnecessary. This view is even more widespread today. The notion of value-free science that it entails is now generally regarded as repudiated.[3] It is evident, as Holzkamp points out, that naive empiricism is incapable even of asking the pertinent questions about relevance and interests, let alone being able to answer them.

It is worth noting that this is the philosophy of science, in more or less explicit form, that historically drove questions of subjectivity from the domain of scientific psychological concern in the ostensible interest of objectivity. The result was the problematic and ambiguous attitude of psychologists – exemplified in John B. Watson, the founder of behaviourism – that either subjectivity did not really exist and it was a mistake to talk about it (in which case, why do we have so much vocabulary relating to it?), or that it existed but lay outside the domain of science as something to be excluded by objective methods (thus creating, in the interest of a reductive monism, the crudest sort of dualist metaphysics). In short, naive empiricism, despite its everyday, common-sense appeal, is a position that (1) is incoherent, and (2) has obstructed the development of an adequate psychology.

LOGICAL EMPIRICISM

There is another version of empiricism, known variously as logical empiricism, logical positivism, or, simply, positivism that theoretically minded psychologists, recognizing the vulnerability of naive empiricism, have adopted more or less offici-ally and that has been influential in shaping both theory and method in psychology in this century.[4] In this position the doctrine of the genetic primacy of experience is abandoned, together with Mill's conception of induction as a principle of the generation of knowledge. It was apparent that science could not begin with experi-ence because it was always necessary to have selection principles embodied in theoretical ideas before it could be known what to observe. Nature by itself could not tell us what we ought to observe. Because of this the induction of generalizations from experience would appear to be logically impossible. Natural laws therefore, according to logical empiricism, are not to be found in nature, which is given to us only in the particulars of space and time and can only be described in singular, here-and-now statements. By contrast, natural laws are defined by their presumed universal validity. They cannot therefore be given to us by our experience of nature but must be formulated by us as assumptions.

Science, according to this view, is a network of statements that form a conceptual pyramid or axiomatic system. It is held together by a principle of internal coherence. The sphere of language in the broadest sense, following Wittgenstein's *Tractatus*, is considered in principle to be non-transcendable. Science consists of statements and *only* of statements. This assumption created considerable difficulty in making clear how the scientific language system is anchored in reality (see Tolman 1991a). For the logical positivists this was presumed to occur through the particular descriptions of sensory events that they called protocol statements. They were never able to fully clarify for others, however, how protocol statements were different in this respect from other kinds of statements.

Out of a concern to avoid the pitfalls of metaphysics the logical empiricists adopted a rigorous criterion for meaningfulness, according to which statements are scientifically meaningful only if they are protocol statements themselves or can be unequivocally deduced from them. The only really scientific problems are those that can be reduced to protocol statements. This empirical criterion of meaningfulness went through several versions and modifications. The form most familiar to psychologists is the operational definition (see Rogers 1991).

Logical empiricism's criterion for the validity of scientific statements differs significantly from that of naive empiricism. Science necessarily takes the form of a statement system in which the statements represented more precise versions of everyday statements. Empirical hypotheses can be logically deduced from the statement system and represented generalizations of the lowest grade of universality within the system. They must fulfil the condition that protocol statements can be deduced from them, that is, that they be operationalizable. The task is then to verify the hypotheses. Whether or to what extent verification occurs depends upon the degree to which predictions derived from the hypotheses are confirmed, that is, the degree to which the observational data agree with the requirements of the hypotheses.

At this point logical empiricism turns to the principle of induction. This is, however, characterized in an essentially different way from that of naive empiricism. It is no longer viewed as a procedure for generating natural laws from experience but only as a principle for establishing the validity of general statements. This means basing validity claims for particular hypothetical predictions on previously acquired observational data: the more a hypothesis has been confirmed in the past, the greater is its predictive value. It becomes clear from this that the inductive procedure cannot yield absolutely conclusive predictions but only probable ones. As a consequence, an attempt was made to formalize the induction procedure with the aid of probability theory.

Logical empiricism represents a distinct and important retreat from the confident expectations of naive empiricism regarding laws of nature and true scientific knowledge. Figuratively speaking, scientists found themselves confined to a cage of statement systems, from which contact with reality would be gained only with the greatest difficulty, if at all. One result has been that attempts to establish the actual validity of scientific propositions have been increasingly neglected, and, instead, scientists who continued on the path of logical empiricism have become preoccupied with systems of rules governing the tautological transformation of one set of statements into another. The most visible manifestation of this in psychology has been the continuing obsession with measurement and statistical analysis.

The problems created by a theory of science that restricts itself to methodological considerations and refuses to deal with matters of substance and interest are even clearer in logical empiricism than in naive empiricism. The naive empiricist notion of empirical constraints that ultimately yield conclusive knowledge is abandoned. Its place is taken by a system in which innumerable internally consistent statement systems are possible and which can be tested empirically. Rules for choosing one internally consistent statement system over another cannot be deduced from the conceptual framework of logical empiricism. The scientist is thus left with a broad latitude for arbitrariness, and, except in procedural matters, scientific activity is removed to a significant degree from rational control.

The unreasonableness of a purely formal, method-oriented theory of science is, however, to a certain extent obscured in logical empiricism by its conception of the verification of hypotheses. In so far as a scientific statement system is supported by verified hypotheses, it can be understood in some sense as true, that is, anchored in reality. It is thus still possible, even if only in a limited way, to claim acquisition of knowledge and truth as the real interest of scientific activity, and allegations of irrationality and arbitrariness in the selection of the contents of research are to some extent countered by appeal to scientific truth. At best, however, this method-centred approach to science creates the appearance of self-justification; it does not help psychology to become more reflective of human subjectivity or more relevant to human needs.

FALSIFICATION THEORY

A third position that has been influential in psychology in the latter half of this century is the falsification theory of Karl Popper (1961, 1966). It is a position based on a critique of logical empiricism's account of the verification of hypotheses. Many psychologists and other social scientists have recognized the problems of verification theory, and have thus naturally been attracted to Popper's seemingly radical critique of it.[5]

For both naive empiricism and logical empiricism the verification of hypotheses depends upon the principle of induction, although what it is presumed to achieve is, as we have already noted, understood quite differently by each of the two positions. It can be demonstrated, however, that the principle of induction, even in the weaker version of logical empiricism, is in fact not tenable. There is no logically defensible reason why the predictive value of a hypothesis should increase to the degree that it has been empirically verified in the past. The related arguments are always circular or question-begging, and, as Popper has shown, appeals to probability theory fail to correct the problem.

On the basis of a critique of the validation version of the induction principle as it formed the basis for hypothesis verification, Popper came to a radical rejection of all claims that science delivers knowledge or truth. He concluded: 'Our science is not knowledge . . .: it can achieve neither truth nor probability' (Popper 1966: 228). In so far as this conclusion is accepted – and Popper's argument, strictly following as it does the canons of deductive logic, *is* compelling – scientists are denied the last possibility of claiming their motives to be purely and simply those of gaining genuine scientific knowledge or truth. Popper repudiated the verification of hypotheses and replaced it with 'falsification'.

Popper's argument was based on classical logic. Science was for him, as it was for the logical empiricists, a system of statements varying in degree of generality in which the connection to reality, however that might be defined, is made by singular statements. He called these singular statements 'basic statements' (his version of protocol statements).

If a basic statement is determined to be true, can it be deduced from that fact that the superordinate system from which the statement has been derived is thereby verified? No, such a conclusion is ruled out because the truth of a particular statement has no implication whatever for the general statements from which it is derived. Popper illustrated this with an example from classical logic: it does not follow logically from 'this swan is white' that 'all swans are white', or that 'some swans are white', or even that 'the probability is now increased that other swans are white'. The verification of a singular judgement says absolutely nothing about the verity of general statements, even when they are formulated in probabilistic terms.

The situation is different, however, when it comes to the falsification of general statements. Although general statements cannot be derived from particular statements, they can be contradicted by them. By virtue of the *modus tollens* of classical logic, the truth of a particular statement can be taken to imply the falseness of a general statement. This naturally assumes that the general statement is formulated as an unqualified all-statement, allowing no exception in its claim to truth. Suppose our statement is that 'all swans are white'. If the basic statement 'this swan is black' can be established as true, the superordinate statement is necessarily false.

On the assumption of an asymmetry between verification and falsification, Popper concluded that empirical scientific theories must be formulated in such a way that makes them most vulnerable to falsification. Theories and theoretical propositions can then be rank-ordered with respect to their degree of falsifiability.

Popper's falsification theory is based on the possibility of specifying criteria for the truth of basic statements, since only when these are established as true can the system of superordinate general statements be considered to be contradicted and thus to be false. But according to Popper (1966: 60ff) the validity of basic statements cannot be decided conclusively but only provisionally, and only if, following the methodological rules of the game, agreement is achieved among different observers regarding its acceptance or rejection. This agreement is easier for some basic statements than for others. If no firm agreement can be achieved on the validity of a particular basic statement, further statements are formulated such as are capable of contradicting the to-be-tested theory until one is found that can be agreed upon according to the rules. Finding such a statement increases the degree of falsifiability of the theory. To the extent that agreement is achieved on the rejection of statements that would contradict the theory, the theory is considered to be provisionally corroborated.

Popper's falsification theory represents, as one can readily see, a further retreat from claims to deliver either scientific knowledge or truth. A scientific statement system that has not yet been falsified is, according to Popper, not to be regarded as 'anchored in reality'. There may be many statement systems that meet this criterion and that stand in greater or lesser agreement with the first one. The facts referred to by the basic statements do not have any authority that is completely independent of the theory under question. They necessarily represent interpretations of reality in light of the same theory. The falsification criterion limits the arbitrariness in retaining scientific statement systems, but it affords no criterion by which to decide what statement systems ought to be formulated and tested. The issue, which of all possible theories about real circumstances ought to be formulated and which hierarchy of values should govern the decision of what is most worthy of investigation, is left by Popper in the domain of the irrational.

Popper saw this problem. But he did not conclude that his theory of science was therefore merely a skeleton that needed to be fleshed out and modified by further philosophical consideration of its focal substance or motivating interests, thus rendering it more susceptible to guidance by reason. Instead he opted for a kind of 'escape into psychology':

> [T]he origin of theories does not appear to be capable or in need of a logical analysis: To the question, how it happens that something new occurs to somebody – whether it be a musical theme, a dramatic conflict, or a scientific theory – might be of interest to psychology, but not to the logical theory of knowledge.
>
> (Popper 1966: 6)

By reducing the theory of science to methodology and logic, Popper excluded from scientific consideration the question of the origin of scientific theories. He thus evaded the related questions about relevance and interests. In so doing, he offered nothing to psychologists concerned with the subjectivity that questions of relevance and interest imply.

THE PROBLEM OF SUBJECTIVITY

These versions of bourgeois philosophy of science in psychology all reveal themselves, despite their particular virtues, to be problematic even on their own terms. In so far as they manage to reconcile their problems within their own constraints, they appear all the more abstract and unreal from the point of view of the ordinary expectations and the actual practice of science. As Holzkamp has repeatedly pointed out, none of them is able to deal with questions that touch either the substantive concerns of science or of relevance in any of its possible senses. This is as true for naive empiricism as for logical empiricism and falsification theory: it only becomes more obvious as we move from one to the next, the deficiency attaining the self-dignifying pretence of a general principle in the last.

What is more important for psychology, however, is the utter failure of these positions to deal adequately with the problem of subjectivity. Their one-sidedness has uniformly sacrificed subjectivity for objectivity. Certainly, if naive empiricism left no room for questions of relevance, it could find no room for subjectivity. The laws with which it was concerned were those of nature inde-pendent of the observing mind and the only knowledge to be valued was knowl-edge of such laws, that is, objective knowledge. The rules were clear: if nature was to reveal its laws to the observer, the latter had to be as non-interfering, as passive, as neutral, as non-subjective as possible. This was the kind of thinking that led already in the nineteenth century to the crudest forms of behaviourism.[6]

One might succeed in demonstrating that naive empiricism, like all empiricisms, was not a materialism in any strict sense, although many of its adherents thought of themselves as materialists and most of its critics have continued to muddy the waters of technical distinction in this regard (cf. Tolman

1991c). Certainly there was enough similarity to philosophical materialism that such a demonstration would often resemble a mere quibble. For logical empiricism, however, the difference is clearer. With the arguable exception of Otto Neurath, adherents of this position were self-consciously not materialists; many of them even denied being realists (e.g. Moritz Schlick); and a few went so far as to openly embrace solipsism (e.g. Rudolph Carnap).[7] With respect to our question about subjectivity, this is certainly not a quibble. The logical empiricists rejected in principle all naive notions of being anchored in mind-independent reality. It was they who accepted the view that the realms of experience as sensation and language were non-transcendable. The 'physicalism' associated with this group is not infrequently understood as equivalent to a kind of materialism but, to those who advocated it, it was anything but materialist. The 'physical' here referred not to physical nature but to physical language, that is, the language of physics. The consequent reduction of psychical phenomena was therefore not a reduction to physical, material events (as it was for reductive materialists like the animal psychologist, Jacques Loeb)[8] but to description in the language of physics. In other words, the prescribed language for protocol statements was simply that of physics.

The irony of all this is that logical empiricism, as its self-confessed solipsists understood, was an essentially subjectivist theory of science. Many of the strict rules they set up for themselves were a direct consequence of this. The only distinction between objective and subjective left to them was a methodological one. The prescriptions regarding what was meaningful and what was not, what counted as science and what did not, etc., were all intended to ward off the indeterminacy of rampant subjectivism. While some theorists, such as the Gestalt psychologists, saw some possibilities in this for the development of something resembling a theory of subjectivity, the majority continued, like the naive empiricists, to treat subjectivity as a pariah to be purged from science as distinct from ordinary, everyday thinking.

Popper's falsification theory basically continued this tendency. It made even less demanding claims about its anchoring. Unlike the logical empiricists who attempted to maintain the constraints of strict order or rationality within the confines of their subjectivist system, Popper gave way to irrationality, the prospect of which had horrified his predecessors. In a sense, falsification theory can be seen as at least a partial *reductio ad absurdum* of logical empiricism. Needless to say, a science of subjectivity, as distinct from a subjectivist science, gains no footing here either.

What these positions all have in common is a restrictive emphasis on individual experience and a sacrifice of the subjectivity of that experience either to objectivity or to the irrationality that the objectivists feared. It might be objected that our critique has overlooked more recent developments in empiricist philosophy. Jäger *et al.* (1979) observe, however, that the 'hard core' of empiricist philosophy, while hardly resembling the more traditional kinds, has come increasingly to rely on the formalisms of physics and mathematics, neither of which has much to say about subjectivity (or about history, which, as we shall see, is important to the understanding of subjectivity). In these positions, therefore, there is even less hope for the individual, stranded, isolated, and abstracted from the societal-historical context which, when acknowledged, is treated as an external and even foreign influence. The individual's subjectivity is correspondingly left with the degraded status of an irrational interference in the development of real knowledge. A psychology developing in this atmosphere must be fraught with the difficulties of dealing with the concrete human subject that we have already noted.

OUTSIDE THE MAINSTREAM: PHENOMENOLOGY

Of course, Holzkamp and the others who undertook to develop a critical psychology at the Free University of Berlin were not the only or the first ones to recognize these problems. In the 1990s we are aware of a burgeoning number of alternative philosophies and psychologies being offered as solutions to the problems we have outlined. Indeed, the constructivism that was occupying Holzkamp during the 1960s was already such an alternative, though he subsequently rejected it because it was found to be vulnerable to many of the same criticisms as empiricism, particularly in regard to its emphasis on internal scientific logic to the exclusion of questions about social and personal relevance.

There are other alternatives that have attracted more positive attention from Critical Psychologists and that we cannot discuss here. One of these, however, can and will be mentioned because of its strong commitment to an adequate account of human subjectivity. This is phenomenology.

There are many distinct positions that can be identified within the genus of phenomenology, most of them acknowledging common origins in the work of Brentano and Husserl and, more recently, Merleau-Ponty, but with significant differences among them. We will confine ourselves to the phenomenology represented in the work of Carl Graumann (1984) because Klaus Holzkamp specifically responded to it.[9]

Holzkamp sees phenomenological analysis as concerned with articulating the irreducible, fundamental structure of the life-world, the human-world interrelation, that we associate with the specifically human mode of existence. Phenomenology starts with the immediately given, human life-world and proceeds to dispense with its particular contents through procedures of bracketing and reduction (Graumann calls this 'structural analysis'). The focal structural characteristic here is the intentional relatedness of the subject to independent objects. 'Intentionality' implies a particular 'me' as a 'centre of intentionality' from which I put myself into relation to a world that exists independently of me, that is, to which I relate.[10]

This 'relating-to' implies as well that any particular other will be experienced by me as 'relating' to me, and thus as another centre of intentionality independent of, but in relation to, me. That is, I will perceive him or her as perceiving me. (First-person pronouns cannot be avoided here. Their use reflects the fact that phenomenology, unlike traditional empiricism, acknowledges the irreducibility of the first person as the starting point for analysis.) Owing to this reciprocal structure our experience is constituted as genuinely social or, more precisely, intersubjective. At the same time, relating-to and intersubjectivity apply as well to my own self: I can relate to myself as a subject, which means that as the other is an other for me, I myself am an other for the other. In the context of this reciprocal relatedness and decentring, intentionality implies the reflexivity of our intersubjective relations to world and to self.

Considering myself as a centre of intentionality, the reality to which I relate will always be made up of what is intended by me. As an experiencer, therefore, I always find myself occupying a particular standpoint with a particular perspective on the world and on my self. This standpoint and perspective then define the limits of my experience. Experience of a world independent of me is possible only to the extent that its features are available to me from my situated standpoint and perspective. Since reality itself will therefore always be greater than anything I have already recognized or actively apprehended, my experience of the world and of my self can be understood as having a horizon beyond which lie unlimited, as yet unexperienced possibilities. Seen in this way, reality becomes for each of us a possibility-space within which we experience and act, and intentionality becomes a possibility-relation to our world and to ourselves. Alternatives and possibilities for action and experience are then defined for any particular person by his or her situated possibility-space. The range and extent of these possibilities for relating to the world and ourselves constitute what we usually regard as our freedom.

Because reality always extends beyond that which I as an individual intend, that is, because the intentional relation is always a possibility-relation, my possibility-space will be limited by that which lies beyond it. In general, it is that which is not (yet) understood or apprehended by me. It is not felt as a mere ignorance, however, but as something that runs against my intentions, as an accidental intrusion by invisible events into my intentionally ordered experience, or as the resistance of reality that compels me to restructure my intentional order in accordance with it.

The anticipatory aspect of my intentional possibility-relation with the world, to others, and to my self can be generalized in my experience as a comprehensive dimension of temporality. My own life, localized in space and time, represents a reference point for the particular intersecting and overlapping temporalities that I experience in the existence of other people and the events and processes of the world. Through the reflection of relating-to back upon myself, my experience of self attains the character of phenomenal historicity in which my past appears as realized or missed opportunities, and my future appears as possibilities that remain more or less open. The unintendable and impenetrable actuality that borders on my possibility-space at any particular time appears in this context as the experienced finiteness of my lifespan: the ultimate, immutable framework for the temporal structuring of my phenomenal biography.

Phenomenology, as described here, is criticized on two counts. First, it tends to abstractness in limiting itself to a structural analysis of experience. An example is the phenomenological conception of freedom. Holzkamp argues, first, that any concretely meaningful conception must include an understanding of consciousness as insight into necessity. The necessities at issue, however, are not given in the structure of subjectivity but of society, and are historically conditioned as the phenomenologically presumed subject-structure is not. Quoting Marx, Holzkamp writes: 'Freedom as insight into necessity is not simply "given" but is rather a "task to be accomplished"' (1984: 25).[11] This requires a concrete theory of history and society that phenomenology does not provide. Following a detailed discussion, which will not be repeated here, Holzkamp finds himself forced to conclude that the individual subjectivity is not, as phenomenology claims, absolutely irreducible (1984: 27). In order to overcome the notions of history and society as mere postulates, which leave us then with an irreducible dualism of subject and object, subjectivity needs itself to be accounted for by a broader theory of history and society of which it is a product and reflection. One of the central methodological starting points for phenomenological analysis, the irreducibility of individual life-world as subjectively experienced is thus seen as ultimately untenable.

A second criticism focuses on a potential indeterminacy contained in phenomenology. Basically this is a problem with the presumed irreducibility of the individual subjective experience (Holzkamp 1984: 10-11). It is possible for a person who adopts the phenomenological point of view to deny that experiential structures are shared. It would be difficult within the framework of the position to refute such a denial. But, of course, there *is* widespread agreement. The problem is that phenomenology does not in itself account for this agreement, and cannot do so without the appropriate theory of history and societal existence.

Holzkamp acknowledges that these criticisms are relatively minor compared to those raised against other philosophies of science. He recognizes the essential correctness of phenomenology as representing a level of analysis required by Critical Psychology. In his view it would be no less inappropriate to apply ideological critiques, such as those to which traditional forms of empiricism are rightly subjected, to phenomenology than to formal logic. Holzkamp sees both phenomenology and logic as 'basic sciences' that provide analytical tools required of any special or substantive science. He thus embraces phenomenological philosophy as part of his overall position. His major criticisms are reserved for those theoretical positions, such as ethnomethodology (see Chapter 3) that, blind to the peculiar one-sidedness of phenomenology, mistakenly think of it as a standpoint that can be developed on its own terms into substantive social science. The impact of phenomenology upon Critical Psychology has been significant and will be recognized in much of its technical terminology (for example, the centrality to Critical Psychology's theory of 'possibility-relations').

DIALECTICAL MATERIALISM

The philosophical position adopted by critical psychology even before it became a self-conscious Critical Psychology was Marxist dialectical materialism.[12] The origins of this choice are found in the educational activities of the Red Cell movement described in the previous chapter.

A definition of dialectical materialism, one that touches economically and fairly on the aspects that will interest us here, is found in Antony Flew's *A Dictionary of Philosophy*:

> A metaphysical position held by many Marxists. It asserts that matter is primary or fundamental, and states general laws governing the motion and development of all matter. As such, it is distinguished from *historical materialism*, which is the Marxist theory of history, dealing with the more particular laws governing the development of human society and thought. In asserting the primacy of matter, dialectical materialists do not advance a reductive theory; they do not assert that everything that exists is *nothing but* matter. Rather, they are concerned to oppose idealism; in their view, matter is not a product of mind, but mind is the highest product of matter. This explains how Marxist historians of philosophy can say that Locke and Spinoza, for example, were materialists. Both these philosophers believed that mind is as real as matter, but they were 'materialists' in the sense that they were not idealists [in the sense of believing that the external world is somehow created by the mind or does not exist independently of the mind]. Dialectical materialists argue that the laws that govern matter are not mechanistic, but are dialectical. Borrowing from Hegel, they assert that these laws are: (a) the transformation of quantity into quality; and conversely, (b) the law of the inter-penetration of opposites . . .; (c) the law of the negation of the negation (that is, the view that reality develops by way of contradiction and the reconciliation of contradiction, the reconciliations producing fresh contradictions).
>
> (Flew 1979: 94–95; material in square brackets added,
> based on Flew's entry on 'idealism' 1979: 160)

Unlike the traditional empiricisms that have effectively dominated psychology for the last century or more of its development, dialectical materialism is a philosophy that directly addresses the problems of relevance and of the relationship between the individual and society. Although not immediately apparent from the description given above, it is also a philosophy that has been consistently concerned with the problem of individual human subjectivity. In this connection Holzkamp (1984: 24) speaks of Marx as a kind of proto-phenomenologist. Most important, the objects of these concerns are expressed in a way that takes them not merely as postulated, but derived or deduced from the principles of the more general theory. For example, in dialectical materialism phenomenology becomes situated as a necessary part of a more general theory of concrete human existence.

Holzkamp has emphasized, however, that an adequate theory of human subjectivity cannot simply be lifted out of existing Marxist philosophy. Although the problem of subjectivity is recognized and concerns about it are expressed, a theory of subjectivity as such is largely lacking in classical Marxist texts. Dialectical materialism is taken, in short, as offering the *potential* of an adequate theory of subjectivity; it remains, however, to be actualized. This is the task that Critical Psychology undertook to complete.

THE CURRENT STATUS OF MARXISM

Has Critical Psychology, with its commitment to Marxism, been overtaken by history? While only a short time ago over a third of the world's population was living in societies that were considered by many to be 'Marxist', this could not reasonably be claimed for many, if any, today. Marxism, it is said, has totally collapsed. Is this true? I believe not.

What we have seen collapse are some societal and ideological systems that became unsustainable for many reasons. Not the least of these has been an enormous hostility exercised against them from the start by powers that ruled the rest of the world. That these societies came to be plagued, however, by domestic incompetence and corruption can hardly be denied. What is even more disappointing is that the apparent efforts made to educate their citizens to socialism failed so utterly. Socialism had been reduced to unquestioning loyalty to the state. In the process, Marxism became rigidified and dogmatized to serve not as a means of understanding real human, historical, life processes, but as a mere justification of the existing order. But if the economies, the political orders, and the indoctrination failed, it seems hardly reasonable to blame Marxism as such. This would be akin to blaming Christianity for the collapse of the feudal system for which it provided the philosophical and ideological justification. Christianity did not collapse with feudalism. The reformations were aimed at purging the Christian establishment and its ideology of its self-serving distortions, and restoring vitality to the religious doctrine with a view to making it more liberating and relevant to the lives of ordinary people. Christianity learned then from its trials and tribulations, and continues to do so today. It does not seem unreasonable to expect the same of another world-view (from which even worldly Christians, such as the liberation theologists of Latin America, have taken inspiration). If the world of human experience was a process in the past that could be informatively described in terms of, say, the law of the transformation of quantity into quality, it seems hardly reasonable to suppose today that, owing to recent events in the 'communist' countries, the world is somehow now better described in different terms. On the contrary, many Marxists (and even some non-Marxists: cf. McLellan 1991) would insist that the best theoretical tool for understanding the 'collapse of communism' is Marxism itself.

Contrary to rumours spread by some gloating opponents of Critical Psychology, then, the philosophical carpet has not been pulled out from under it.

Chapter 3

Social-historical theory

Although psychologies may be mainly concerned with the behaviour or mental functioning of individuals, they all presuppose some sort of social-historical theory, which, in turn, supports the theoretical form in which the psychology presents itself. Even if the social and historical contexts of the individual are thought to be irrelevant, that in itself constitutes a social-historical theory and will have a shaping influence on the consequent psychology.

In its critique of this aspect of bourgeois psychology, Critical Psychology, consistent with its adoption at the philosophical level of dialectical materialism, takes as its basis *historical materialism*. The critique has two aspects. The first is a *conceptual* critique which focuses on, among other things, bourgeois psychology's failure to consider the relevance of social class and class antagonisms, and its reduction of societal relations to unmediated social interaction; that is, its treatment of the other people in our lives simply as another class of stimulus object.

The second aspect of the critique is *methodological* and is directed at the way in which psychology's methods reproduce the individualist assumptions and dominance relations of bourgeois ideology, and its consequent inability to produce an understanding of the person in capitalist class relations, such as people would require in order for them consciously to take charge of their lives and collectively alter those relations (Holzkamp 1983: 27).

'SOCIAL' VERSUS 'SOCIETAL'

The reader will have noticed the appearance of the word 'societal' where 'social' might otherwise be expected. Holzkamp speaks of his interest in *societal* processes and indicates that he will criticize bourgeois psychology for its reduction of such processes to *social* interaction. Since this is a distinction that is more common in German than in English, a few words of explanation are in order.

In English the word 'societal' has a strained and artificial sound to it. It is almost never encountered in English-language psychology and social science. Indeed, the blanket term 'social science' is already an indicator of this. In German, however, there are two words that are commonly translated as 'social', namely, *sozial* and *gesellschaftlich*. This common translation, however, over-looks a distinction that is especially important for Holzkamp and the Critical Psychologists. The word *sozial* refers to social existence in the broadest sense of the word. Thus we speak of social animals and social organizations of animals. Humans and their organizations are social too. We have social events like parties and live in communities. But humans and their organizations are not *merely* social. Animal social relations tend to be largely rooted in the biology of the species in question. We can predict with considerable accuracy how rats, lions, and dogs will interact, develop dominance hierarchies, raise their young, etc., on the basis of knowing their species alone. It does not seem to matter much whether these rats, lions, or dogs live in Canada, Argentina, or China. It also does not seem to matter much whether we are speaking of rats, lions, and dogs that are living now or lived a thousand years ago.

Considering humans in these spatio-temporal contexts, however, we arrive at quite different conclusions. The ways in which we interact, dominate one another, and raise our young, reflect very much where and when we live. The information that guides us in these kinds of action is not so much carried in our biology, although that is unquestionably important, as in our *culture*. The organized groupings of human beings that do the actual carrying of culture are called *societies*. Because the nature of the information that is important to us for survival is cultural, it is quite labile in the sense that it can change dramatically and rapidly from time to time and place to place, or from society to society. This is what accounts for both cultural differences and for *history*, in contradistinction to biological evolution, as the way in which we conceptualize changes in culture over time. Put briefly, humans have cultural existences while rats do not; humans live in society while rats live in social relations; humans have history while rats depend on biological evolution. This makes humans very different, indeed *quali-tatively* different, from all other animal species. This is the difference between *sozial* and *gesellschaftlich*, the difference between 'social' and 'societal'.[1]

From Holzkamp's point of view the distinction is essential because, as we shall see, what is distinctly human about psychological processes, most especi-ally subjectivity, is precisely that they are societal, not merely social. The problem of subjective interests does not arise with rats or even with subhuman primates in the way that it does with humans, and, as experience in any social movement like the German student movement clearly demonstrates, subjective interests are concerns that belong to societal and historical existence; subjectivity represents a category that is simultaneously scientific and political.[2]

THE CRITIQUE IN OUTLINE

Holzkamp formulates his problem in the following way:

> The springboard for all controversy about an adequate understanding of the problem of subjectivity and its ontogenesis is the set of questions concerning

the definition of the *relationship between subjectivity and the societal character of individuals*: is individual subjectivity reducible to societal relations, or are these something that stand independent of and in opposition to it? If subjectivity is something independent, then how is its *difference* to be reconciled with the nevertheless existing *connection* between the individual's sociality and subjectivity? Or, more particularly, if the result of ontogenesis is in some sense the 'societalized' or 'socialized' subject, how then is the *individual societalization* that is achieved to be precisely defined? What is the *initial state of early childhood* from which the societalization process begins and what is the *necessary course governing the ontogenetic transition* from the initial state to the final result of individual societalization?

(Holzkamp 1979: 12)

It is questions like these that must be asked and answered if a critical theory of human subjectivity is to be achieved; it is questions like these that bourgeois psychology tends not to ask, let alone answer.

More is required, however, than simply asking the right questions. Methods must be available for answering such questions in non-arbitrary ways that would count as yielding real knowledge. Here, Holzkamp takes his cue from Marx and Hegel who maintained that explanation was deductive, not from arbitrary premises, but from real states of affairs:

The premises from which we begin are not arbitrary ones, not dogmas, but real premises from which abstraction can only be made in the imagination. They are the real individuals, their activity and the material conditions under which they live, both those which they find already existing and those produced by their activity. These premises can thus be verified in a purely empirical way.

(Marx and Engels 1846/1970: 42)

Referring to the questions just listed, Holzkamp echoes the Hegelian-Marxist understanding:

If the answers to such questions are to have scientific character, then we must be able to explicate their *context of understanding*, that is, the *principle of deduction* by which one arrives at the particular determinants of the relationship between subjectivity and societality.

(Holzkamp 1979: 12)

The German word here is *Ableitung*, which could mean either 'derivation' or 'deduction'. The former is weak, however, and detracts from the origins and justifications of this idea in classical German philosophy, particularly in Hegel. It is not to be confused with either the merely 'formal' deduction of classical logic or, what is derived from it, the deduction of empiricist psychology's hypothetico-deductive method (cf. Holzkamp 1983: 68fn). As implied in the quotation from Marx and Engels, deduction refers to revealing the necessity of a process of development, either of one state from another or of an idea or concept of the state from the state itself. This latter deduction is, of course, the result of human activity with objects, as when a child comes to understand elasticity by playing with elastic bands.

The critique of bourgeois social science thus becomes directed at its methodology: 'both "psychology" and "sociology" lack any method for the deduction of scientifically grounded determinants of the relationship between subjectivity and individual societality' (Holzkamp 1979: 13).

BOURGEOIS PSYCHOLOGY

Holzkamp's critique of traditional bourgeois psychology begins with the observation that it 'isolates individuals from the concrete societal-historical contexts of their lives, understands them as abstract units of behaviour in a reductive environment stripped of its historical determination' (Holzkamp 1979: 14). This implies what Holzkamp calls an 'anthropology of the abstract-isolated individual', a set of assumptions about human nature found hidden in virtually all of traditional social science. These assumptions have found no clearer expression than in the 'nomothetic variable-model'[3] that forms the unreflected foundation of experimental psychology's methodology. According to this model, research consists of the testing of assumptions about the connections between experimentally produced initial conditions (independent variables) and measures of the subjects' behavioural responses (dependent variables). Individuals are effectively treated here as 'switchboxes' that transform the initial conditions into behaviour patterns according to presumably general laws, which may vary with the particular substantive theory. The conditions under which people live are represented in the theoretical concepts only to the extent that they exercise an *immediate* influence on the individuals. Determinants that lie beyond the immediate conditions of organismic change, but which may characterize the objective constitution of the individuals' life-worlds, tend to be disregarded. Similarly, the ways in which individual lives express themselves are only understood to the extent that they appear as the result of immediate influences on the organism and as modified by the 'switchbox'.

These understandings are reflected in the way in which psychologists speak of their subject matter as 'variables' and the connections they make – that get 'switched' – through the organism. Such a language manages already at a basic conceptual level to excise the historical-societal concreteness of individual modes of living and action, and thus makes it virtually impossible for psychology to grasp the real connections between individual lives and societal activity that exist beyond the limits of the immediate situational and biographical frameworks (cf. Holzkamp 1978: 164ff). What is portrayed for us instead is an abstracted individual, reduced to one or more response measures as they correlate with a world likewise reduced to one or more situational variables.

With respect to our present concerns, this means that the conceptual system of psychology already excludes the societal character of individuals as a factor at the level of its very foundation – e.g. by virtue of the way in which it conceptualizes its subject matter. The consequence of this is that the relationship between subjectivity and societality is rendered inaccessible, even unimaginable, from the start. A psychology that defines its subject matter in terms of variables is, in short, not prepared even to ask the right questions, let alone give us their answers (Holzkamp 1979: 14–15).

A curious thing about this state of affairs is that it is not denied by traditional psychologists. It is seen rather as a necessary consequence of the scientific division of labour. As the definition of psychology given in virtually any current textbook will reveal, psychology is concerned with individual matters (formerly behaviour, now behaviour and cognition) and not with matters relating to society, which are regarded as the province of sociology, economics, and political science. Matters from these disciplines relating to society, however, can be and often are brought into psychology but they have to be first translated into the language of variables. For example, socio-economic status, understood as a measurable variable, can be used as an independent variable in a psychological experiment about behavioural or cognitive processes. Concepts like this can also appear as dependent variables, as in the case of attitudes or so-called prosocial behaviours. But the very fact that such societal dimensions must first be translated into the variable language of psychology suggests already that they are in themselves *meaningless* for the purpose of *psychological* explanation:

> The laws by which . . . the independent variables are transformed into the dependent variables thus appear as *ahistorical invariances* that are totally indifferent to whether or how they might be provided with societal-historical substance. Individuals in the net of immediate influences and their law-governed links to behaviour patterns are here regarded *on their own terms* as *ultimate*; consideration of the conditions of societal life and the like are treated as extraneous.
>
> (Holzkamp 1979: 15)

This criticism extends not only to general experimental psychology but also to so-called social psychology, in which it becomes perhaps even more apparent. This psychology is also in the thrall of nomothetic variable-model thinking. Other people are accordingly introduced as independent variables, and therefore as simply the providers of initial conditions for the behaviour of the subject. This may, however, be complicated at times by the recognition of a kind of reciprocity or interaction. Even here, however, only the immediate influences of individuals on the behaviour of one another in dyads or groups are taken into consideration. Lawful connections between the recorded influences and resulting behaviour are treated as ahistorical invariances, and the societal, historical dimensions of the observed 'social' behaviour are excluded. Alternatively, if they are brought into consideration they are translated into the language of variables and thus stripped of their societal, historical concreteness. Treated as variables, the societal, historical dimensions of individual activity become eliminable from and irrelevant to psychological laws, which are presumed to have existence independent of them. The interpersonal relational structures investigated by social psychology are thus understood as constructed from independent, immediate, and reciprocal influences of individuals upon one another (and their lawful transformation into behaviour patterns) and as isolated (or in principle isolable) from the conditions of actual societal life. Social psychology does not challenge the limits imposed upon it by the ahistoric, nomothetic variable-model (Holzkamp 1979: 16).

Traditional psychology is consequently rendered by its own conceptual and methodological presuppositions incapable of grasping the relationship between the individual and society that is so essential to understanding subjectivity. Psychology postulates the individual as abstract and isolated (its hidden anthropology). The discipline's entire theoretical structure is based on this postulate. As a result, it is constitutionally incapable of producing any data or insight on anything outside the artificial limits imposed by this anthropology. It becomes a self-confirming position within a carefully shielded world of independent variables, dependent variables, and all the various forms of statistical analysis that are used to relate them in a way that is as abstract as the way in which they were originally produced.

STRUCTURAL-FUNCTIONAL SOCIOLOGY

Sociological positions that claim no interest in individuals as such and consequently focus their attention exclusively on social structures and processes as wholes (like the state and religion) need not concern us here. The most prominent positions in the discipline, both the one at the centre of the mainstream and many lying nearer the periphery, do express theoretical concern for individuals and, on the surface at least, offer more promising prospects than can be found in psychology. Holzkamp examines three of these that he considers representative of sociology in the latter half of the twentieth century and finds them falling short of their promises. The positions we shall examine briefly are the structural-functionalism of Talcott Parsons, who exerted a formative influence on US sociologists, and two phenomenologically oriented theories: ethnomethodology and symbolic interactionism.

Talcott Parsons' early critiques of positivism and utilitarianism focused on many of the same problems as Holzkamp's critique of empiricist psychology, namely reductionism, mechanism, and the failure to grasp the structural nature of society. The main influences on Parsons' thought were Weber, Pareto, and Durkheim, who themselves were influenced by the same anti-empiricist, German idealist tradition of thought to which Critical Psychology traces its historical roots.

While Parsons' principal concern was to develop a comprehensive theory of society, he understood that this could not be accomplished without a simultaneous understanding of the roles played by individual actors within the societal structure. Lewis Coser summarized the central components of Parsons' theory of society as human action as follows:

(a) actors, capable of voluntary striving, emphatically not behaving and reacting bodies; (b) goals that these actors were striving for; (c) choices between alternative means these actors were using in their pursuits; (d) situational constraints coming from both biological and environmental conditions, which set bounds to the selection of means and the accomplishment of ends; and (e) sets of norms and values that channelled the actors' choices of both means and ends.

(Coser 1977: 563)

Parsons also emphasized the role of socialization in the development of the individual personality through identification, internalization, and role-modelling. This part of his theory reflected strong Freudian influences.

Holzkamp maintains, however, that, despite Parsons' intentions, 'a genuine *sociological* conception of individual societalization processes is totally absent' (Holzkamp 1979: 21). Instead, what one finds is that psychoanalytic ideas are simply imported into the sociological theory. Holzkamp describes the result:

Two kinds of concepts are thus made to confront one another: *sociological* ones for characterizing the social or cultural system, values, norms, institutions, roles, etc., and describing individual processes, and *psychological* ones like value-dispositions, identification, role model, internalization, and superego.

(Holzkamp 1979: 21)

Holzkamp goes on to note that to the latter ideas Parsons adds 'certain echoes' of learning theory like reward and punishment (positive and negative sanction). What this indicates to Holzkamp is that Parsons unreflectingly

presupposes and reproduces the scientific division of labour, according to which psychology is responsible for the individual and sociology for society, and thus fully adopts psychology's problematic emphasis on the imaginary individual as abstract and isolated from the conditions of societal life.

(Holzkamp 1979: 21)

The result is a kind of interdisciplinary *eclecticism* in which the individual and societal aspects of human activity, having been wrenched apart by the so-called scientific division of labour, are now added back together and externally related to one another. Socialization is the focal process that then comes to be seen as the link between the individual and society. 'The question about how individual subjectivity is related to a person's becoming a societal being . . . remains, as before, unanswered' (Holzkamp 1979: 21).

The problem here is that the psychological individual is conceived of, whether intentionally or not, as an essentially *biological* being equipped with drives and needs, who is now thrust into society. Socialization processes are then required to transform this biological-psychological being into a societal one.

The *psychological* conceptions by which human individuality is supposed to be understood are not related to the *sociological* conceptions of society in any deductive way; there can therefore be no talk of a scientific understanding of the relationship between individual and society.

(Holzkamp 1979: 22)

As Holzkamp summarizes the problem, it does not matter whether one assumes with Parsons that the individual is adaptable to the pre-existing demands of society through a process of socialization, thus creating a potential harmonious, friction-free relationship between the two, or, like Freud, that the individual and society are unalterably opposed such that society can only frustrate and oppress the individual. However different in appearance, all such positions postulate the separate existence of society and individual, and then seek to discover the means by which the two become related to each other. 'It is evident', writes Holzkamp, 'that with premises such as these *no scientifically grounded deduction* of the individual–society relationship can be achieved' (1979: 22). Why, for instance, should the individual be socializable at all? What is it about individual drives that they come into opposition to *the* society and are repressed by it? Given the anthropology of the isolated individual, we are left only to postulate answers to questions like these. The assumptions on which our psychology and sociology are based preclude scientific answers (cf. Holzkamp 1979: 22).

SYMBOLIC INTERACTIONISM AND ETHNOMETHODOLOGY

Symbolic interactionism and ethnomethodology are more recent positions in sociology that adopt a more phenomenological basis. They have explicitly emphasized the more subjective aspects of socialization such as problems of interpretation and meaning. Like Parsons, they, too, are linked to the German idealist, in contradistinction to empiricist tradition, although by somewhat different routes, such as through Mead and the phenomenologists.

The initial presupposition of these positions is the existence of irreducible individual needs. These form the basis of all interpretations of the self and world that ultimately constitute the meaning systems through which further interpretations are made. Meanings and needs form the basis of expectations which guide action. Individuals are dependent upon one another for the satisfaction of their needs, thus necessitating a commonality of expectations. This occurs through the process of *symbolic interaction* (or something comparable) which is aimed at achieving common interpretations. This brings individual needs into the social sphere and causes modifications of interpretation which, through compromise, achieve a reciprocity of understandings that make possible an optimal satisfaction of participant needs. Society plays various roles here. It provides the language for interpretation and communication. It is the object of interpretation through which social relations take on special meanings for the subjects. Further, it provides for each individual a kind of pre-existing, autonomous system of interpretations and expectations. All this culminates in a view of society as something resisting the interpretations and expectations of individuals. Society allows only a certain amount of leeway for these and thus can create obstacles to communication, common meanings, and agreements. The optimal satisfaction of needs can consequently become oppressive.

Regarding the relationship between subjectivity and society, Holzkamp (1979: 23–24) identifies two tendencies in symbolic interactionism and ethnomethodology: first, societal relations are understood as patterns of immediate interactive processes of interpretation, communication, and agreement that are ultimately grounded in individual needs and expectations. This does not present the *relationship* between subjectivity and society in any new form. All that is accomplished here is a partial subjectification of society by a fundamentally non-societal individual who only secondarily comes into interaction with other similarly non-societal individuals. This reduction of societal relations to the immediate reciprocal influences of individuals on each other is simply another version of social psychology, which, though lacking the nomothetic pretensions of Parsons' structural-functionalism, remains vulnerable to all the criticisms we have already raised against that position.

Second, society is reduced to individual processes of interaction and communication. In so far as it is not subjectified as a supraindividual system of interpretations, society functions solely as the *negative side* of the personal interpretative system, and thus appears as a kind of foreign, blind, and meaningless resistance to the meaning-giving activity of human subjectivity. The total separation of subjective and societal determinants is consequently reproduced but, as it were, from the other side. The restriction and obstruction of subjective and intersubjective systems of interpretation and expectation by society consequently appears as an *inexplicable accident*.

Holzkamp concludes that, although some interesting and important moves of a phenomenological sort are made by symbolic interactionism and similar positions, they do not bring us significantly closer to a scientific understanding of the relationship between society and subjectivity.

MAIN POINTS OF THE CRITIQUE SUMMARIZED

What we encounter over and over again in traditional (as well as less traditional) bourgeois theory is the hidden anthropology of the abstract-isolated individual. Most psychological theories make no attempt at all to overcome this anthropology, failing even to recognize it as a problem. They fall back on the traditional division of labour among the sciences, acknowledging no responsibility to account for society or to show the necessary relationships between the individuals they claim as theirs and the society in which those individuals live. Many sociological theories adopt an inverted position. They study social processes of which individuals are admittedly a part but they do not therefore feel obliged to give an account of the individual, let alone of the individual's subjectivity. This leaves a third group of theories that recognize the problem and seek to account for the individual–society relationship but, as we have seen, succeed only in underscoring it. In their attempt to bring the two levels together, the *necessary* interconnections implied by the *deduction* that Holzkamp feels is required are never exposed. The result is a kind of individual–society dualism that abstracts and reifies both; laws of interaction (*à la* Descartes) are then invoked to bring the two sides back together. The result is eclecticism, a position that recognizes the two sides as necessary but fails to grasp the nature of their necessary interconnection.

The implication of this is not a mere theoretical inelegance, but a fundamental inability to grasp human subjectivity, the key to which, according to Holzkamp, lies in the necessary interconnection between the individual and society. We will see this more clearly perhaps in the next chapter, which deals with the level of special psychological theories. Greater clarity will come, however, when we can see a concrete alternative, to which Parts III and IV of this book will be devoted.

HISTORICAL MATERIALISM

The German Critical Psychologists opted for dialectical materialism at the philosophical level of analysis. At the level of societal-historical theory they therefore adopt the theory deriving from that philosophy that deals with society and history, namely historical materialism. This was Marx's theory of human society. It can be distinguished by two important features: (1) its emphasis on history as a process, the understanding of which allows the deduction or explanation of existing circumstances; and (2) its basic acceptance of a dialectical unity of the individual and society, which holds the potential for overcoming the anthropology of the abstract individual (and the abstract society) that Holzkamp's critique reveals to be characteristic of the social sciences.

Historical materialism provides the basis for Holzkamp's conclusion that the essential cause of the problems of traditional psychology and sociology that result in the opposition of subjective and societal determinants is the lack of an adequate deductive basis for analysing their relationship. How then is such a deductive basis to be found?

According to Holzkamp (1979: 29–34), a necessary step in this direction is to bring into our account a consideration of the historical development of bourgeois society as disclosed by the analysis described in *The Critique of Political Economy* and *Capital*. Marx's critique was not merely a description of the 'anatomy' of the capitalist mode of production: it achieved a qualitatively new level of societal analysis distinguished by the fact that the *subject of knowledge* was brought into the analysis in a significant way. The subject of the analysis of bourgeois society – because it is an aspect of bourgeois society – is also historically defined.

Bourgeois society must be understood in terms of its own laws of motion and development, that is, of production and reproduction. If the subject of knowledge is an aspect of this motion and development, it is not externally opposed to the societal processes of production and reproduction but is defined by and defines it. It is the conscious being of the actual life-process. What must be grasped from the analysis of bourgeois society in its various forms and phases is how scientific consciousness as the subject of knowledge can be an integral part of the societal process and at the same time rise above the limitations thus placed upon it.

If we want to understand this connection concretely, we must start from the premise provided by the historical essence of bourgeois society, namely, as Marx was able to show in his analyses, that the societal labour that serves as the basis of society's survival takes the form of private producers working independently of each other. Because in capitalist societies the societal products of labour are produced for exchange in the market, they take the form of commodities, and within societal relations individuals appear in the seemingly non-societal form of private commodity owners linked to each other by money as the universal common denominator. Commodities are exchanged on the basis of their value, that is, the objectified form of the societally average labour time necessary for their production. Everything and anything can be quantitatively compared in terms of its abstract *exchange value*, thus making possible the exchange of goods. Exchange value is contrasted with the *use value* created by concretely useful labour that gives the commodity its quality.

Behind the relations of exchange in the 'sphere of circulation' stands the 'production sphere' in which societal cooperation is divided into the private owners of the means of production and their agents, on the one hand, and those who possess only their labour power and survive only by access to the means of production, on the other. Workers come, apparently of their own free will, to capitalists in the sphere of circulation as free and private owners, that is, as owners of labour power. In the sphere of circulation the relations of exchange are applied absolutely to human labour power. The contract concluded in apparent freedom between workers and capitalists mystifies the actual state of affairs, which is that in order for the workers to maintain their individual existences they *must* sell their labour power to, and produce surplus value for, the capitalists who own the means of production. And they must do this according to the rules of the capitalist relations of production.

Beneath this relationship of seemingly free and equal 'private parties' in the marketplace lies a relationship of societal exploitation. Those who are dependent on wages are subject to the domination of capital and are not regarded by capital as human subjects, but are simply hired or fired as means for creating surplus value. This contradiction between workers appearing to be free agents and their actual lack of freedom forms the basis of bourgeois ideology that one-sidedly portrays these exploitive interpersonal relationships as those of free and equal 'private parties' in the sphere of circulation.

The specific character of the societal in its bourgeois form, therefore, is that it presents itself in terms of privacy. 'Privacy can be understood as a specific societal form of the self-negation of the societal' (Haug 1977: 81). Thus

the motion and development of bourgeois society are defined by this fundamental contradiction . . . between organic, societal production and a simultaneous inorganic, atomistic chaos, that is, societal production under the domination of private ownership. . . . Just as necessarily as the capitalist mode of production yields this fundamental contradiction, it also creates contradictions at the specific level of conscious action in the working class, in its organizations and its struggles. Thus at the same time the capitalist mode of production produces its exploited human element . . . it also produces the increasingly self-conscious element of a higher societal formation.

(Haug 1977: 82)

THE PRODUCTION OF CONSCIOUSNESS

Contradictions in the capitalist mode of production give rise to contradictory forms of consciousness as 'conscious being', simultaneously determined by and determining it. The category that provides the key to a scientific understanding of the consciousness that arises spontaneously with bourgeois economic formations is the category of 'objective thought-forms' (Marx 1867/1971: 90).[4] Because individuals must actively negotiate their lives in particular economic formations, they learn the objective rules for acting within those formations. Their consciousness is not autonomous nor should it be understood as more than what it actually is, namely, being consciously active in a particular economic formation.

From the point of view of living and acting (practising) in these formations, thinking is *necessarily* subject to the logic of the particular formation. It must be thus subjected if the individual is to practise successfully in it. This subjection of consciousness, therefore, is not a starting point, but an end result. Through it the economic formation shapes the objective forms of thought. Being subject in this way to immediate economic practice, thought in this form is always 'appropriate'. It is consequently not inappropriate from the standpoint of the everyday practice of exchange to understand value as something reified or as a relation between things; that is precisely how it works. The consciousness that is functional *in* a particular economic form becomes false when it generalizes to a supposed consciousness *about* things and relations. When this happens consciousness remains not only shaped by the economic form; it remains unaware that it is thus shaped, with the result that it spontaneously and unconsciously reproduces it (cf. Haug 1977: 83).

The explanation of the spontaneous, everyday consciousness in bourgeois society as structured by such objective thought-forms sheds light both on its subordinated, coopted 'correctness' and on its necessary 'falseness'. Marx thus speaks of the *necessarily false consciousness*, in which not only the false is emphasized but, more importantly, the fact that it is *necessary*, given the context of people's everyday lives (cf. Haug 1977: 83f).

The objective, contradictory thought-forms that arise from the capitalist mode of production are manifested in the life-practice of individuals as thinking *in* the seemingly private forms of societal life. The latter are blindly reproduced in individual consciousness, consequently 'naturalizing' them and giving them the appearance of being characteristic of human life in general. They are also manifested in societal practice as thinking *about* these forms, thereby creating the possibility of seeing beyond the privacy that conceals the historical form of exploitation. These alternative modes of thinking are also reflected in science, where the opposition between thinking *in* and thinking *about* the private forms of the capitalist mode of production appears as an opposition between bourgeois science and critical science. The latter thus raises everyday practice to a higher level of 'methodical' consciousness that seeks the kind of coherence that can feed back into practice, changing and extending it.

TOWARDS A CRITICAL SCIENCE

Science in bourgeois society is uncritical when it spontaneously reproduces the presumably natural forms of bourgeois existence. But it cannot restrict itself to reproduction alone. It is the nature and societal function of science to go beyond mere reproduction, that is, to press against and go beyond barriers. Bourgeois science must then, depending on the historical situation and the object of study, extend existing societal limits. But we have to distinguish between barriers or limits *in* bourgeois society and those *of* bourgeois society. It is the latter that science cannot violate without transforming itself into critical science (cf. Haug 1977: 86f). Critical science differs from bourgeois science in that it cannot exist as an ideal parallel to private appropriation.

> [It] is only possible as a component of a consciously anticipatory, comprehensive human appropriation of the historical product. To understand historical creation scientifically requires a corresponding creation in history. Why not consciously *make* that which is *consciously* made?
>
> (Haug 1977: 86)

Critical science thus arises out of a particular developmental state of bourgeois society and its contradictions. It is, however, not subjected to bourgeois forms in its thinking and practice: it takes these precisely as the objects of its thought and proceeds in its practice beyond the limits they impose.

On the basis of this understanding of the critique of political economy, we can specify the general character of traditional psychology and sociology as bourgeois more precisely: these sciences are distinguished by their thinking *in* the forms of bourgeois private relations. Their possibilities for real knowledge, however much they may have succeeded in overcoming the barriers *in* bourgeois society, find their absolute and insurmountable limit in the relations of privacy which are the barriers *of* bourgeois society and which these sciences reproduce. The limits can be defined even more precisely for bourgeois psychology and sociology in as much as they take human individuals as their object:

> The subject of research is first of all subjected to the immediate forms given to each and every individual by society as his or her *social space*. . . . The

subject of research is an inhabitant of the same world and finds him- or herself in the same situation. . . . For psychologists, who take other subjects as their research object, the problem becomes particularly acute. Being subjected to the same determining forms as their research subjects, they view them through, as it were, the same defining forms. This subjection to a way of seeing necessarily remains unconscious; becoming conscious of it requires a breakthrough. It is precisely this taken-for-grantedness with which things are viewed that is the symptom of the subjection to these forms.

(Haug 1977: 78)

Because of their blind reproduction of bourgeois forms of privacy, bourgeois psychology and sociology can, in so far as they deal with human individuals, only investigate individual subjects as they are defined by bourgeois forms, that is, as private parties. Because they are not conscious of bourgeois society's historical definition of the forms of privacy, they necessarily equate 'private parties' with human beings in general.

The covert anthropology of the abstract-isolated individual can now be seen in terms of the preceding analysis as grounded in the unconscious mental reproduction of the real *abstractness* and *isolatedness* of individuals *in* bourgeois society. The isolation of individuals from the concrete societal and historical contexts of their lives is made manifest here as the mental reproduction of their non-societal appearing, self-negating sociality as it is historically determined by bourgeois forms of privacy. It consequently becomes clear that the conceptual separation and external opposition of *the* individual and *the* society in bourgeois psychology and in related conceptions of bourgeois sociology are, in fact, the unconscious theoretical expression of the actual separation of the private and societal processes in the reality of bourgeois society. The inability of bourgeois psychology and sociology to deal adequately with the relationship between the subjectivity and sociality of individuals is, therefore, only the scientific reflection of the fact that bourgeois private individuals do constitute the negation of their societal contexts, and find themselves within the actual contingency and turbulence of the conflicting interests of independent producers (cf. Holzkamp 1979: 33–34).

IMPLICATIONS FOR PSYCHOLOGY

Specific theories in psychology, lacking a reflection of adequate knowledge *about* society and history as such, will also fail to grasp their own embeddedness in societal modes of thinking, particularly ideology. We can expect, therefore, to find that psychological theories are not only blind to their own ideological nature, but actively reproduce in ideal form the historical relations in which they are themselves produced. This being the case, it would be a mistake to see the essential error of these theories as a failure correctly to represent reality: their error is to take bourgeois reality, however faithfully they represent it, as *the* reality.

It follows that theories like this cannot serve as a basis for criticizing existing societal relations. As the Critical Psychologists put it, their criticism will always be confined to issues *in* bourgeois society; they cannot be *about* that society.[5] Historical materialism gives us the theory *about* bourgeois society that creates the potential for the development of genuinely Critical Psychological theory. It is now to specifically psychological theories that we turn in the next chapter.

Chapter 4

Specific psychological theories

If our critiques at the levels of philosophy and theory of society are on the right track, the critique of specific psychological theories should prove to be a straightforward matter. The inadequacies at these two fundamental levels have consequences for the social sciences: (1) for lack of an adequate understanding of society and history, they blindly but necessarily reproduce in some theoretical form or another the actually isolated individual in bourgeois society as an abstract-isolated individual; and (2) they utterly fail to grasp subjectivity as a manifestation of the concrete relationship between the individual and society. This being the case, we can hardly expect to find these faults remedied (miraculously, as it were) at the level of special theories. On the contrary. Having now been alerted to the theoretical problem and its nature, we should only expect to see their faults more clearly.

This point cannot be illustrated here from a survey of the entire spectrum of psychological theory. The focus will be restricted to two mainstream positions, behaviourism and cognitive psychology, and to psychoanalysis, which though peripheralized by academic psychology remains nevertheless important. These three positions represent sufficiently different views within the spectrum to illustrate the pervasiveness of the problem.

It should be acknowledged that psychologies have existed that are less vulnerable to our criticisms than the ones we have chosen (indeed, we shall encounter some interesting ambivalence already in the case of psychoanalysis). One example is the *Völkerpsychologie* of Wilhelm Wundt, which has recently received some renewed critical attention (see, for example, Danziger 1983, 1990; Maiers 1988; Holzkamp 1991b: 86–88). Another is the work of Lewin prior to his 'Americanization' (see, for example, de Rivera 1976; Stivers and Wheelan 1986; Danziger 1990: 173–178; Holzkamp 1991a: 79). These positions will not be examined here, but it is useful to note that their somewhat less problematic nature (from our point of view) is not unrelated to the German idealist background that they share with Marxism and German Critical Psychology.

The final part of this chapter will be devoted to a methodological problem that is common to mainstream bourgeois psychological theories and related to their inability to comprehend subjectivity. This is theoretical indeterminacy, the inability to resolve differences among seemingly competing specific theories (e.g. between learning theory and psychoanalytic accounts of neurosis). It is, as we shall see, a problem that must be solved if we are to break through the anthropology of the abstract-isolated individual, and its solution will be derived, like that of the problem of subjectivity, from methods based on the assumptions of historical materialism.

BEHAVIOURAL-FUNCTIONAL PSYCHOLOGY

There are good historical reasons for separating behaviourist and functionalist theories in psychology. We can point to slightly different histories, differing degrees of metaphysical tolerance, and certain specific claims that distinguish the two positions. There are also good historical reasons, however, for putting them together. Certainly by the 1940s, if not earlier, the real differences that could be found in a comparison, say, of John Dewey and John Watson, had effectively dissolved into mere differences of terminology. Woodworth's insistence on the S-O-R formula in place of the more arid S-R formula did not mark an *essential* difference between the positions, nor did Woodworth's greater tolerance for teleological language.

By the middle of the century, mainstream, bourgeois, American psychology, the kind that would become almost universal after World War II, was through and through behaviouristic, no matter how it labelled itself. This is nowhere clearer than in the universal adoption of behaviourist methods based on independent variables (stimulus conditions), dependent variables (behavioural responses), and the reliability of their connections as assessed by a variety of statistical techniques representing variations on regression analysis (correlation coefficient, t-tests, analyses of variance, regression analyses, etc.). Differences among the now academically accepted psychological theories came to turn on matters such as which variables deserved attention, how they might be measured, and what kind of language should be allowed for talking about the resulting correlations (e.g. hypothetical constructs versus intervening variables).

In these now-familiar methods alone we can easily see the ideological anthropology of the isolated individual at work. The subject of a normal experiment is selected (ostensibly) at random. He or she is placed into as sterile an environment as possible (called 'experimental situation'). One or more measures are extracted from the subject, whereupon the subject is discharged. The measures from each subject, already an abstraction of a rather high degree, are then added together, and averages, means or medians, are calculated. The test of the hypothesis (only the null hypothesis is really tested) is accomplished by comparing differences between group averages (accounted variance) with differences among the subjects (error variance). From the first abstraction we thus move to even more rarefied abstractions. The actual movement is from the very concrete level of an actual human life to a level of abstraction at which no concrete individual existence is any longer recognizable. It is no extreme claim that our methods first isolate the individual and then abstract him or her beyond recognition. As already mentioned earlier, social psychology does not improve the picture. The use of another person or interaction with a group as an independent variable does not constitute a recognition or taking into account of the societal nature of the individual.

With the picture of the standard psychological experiment before us, another important feature becomes obvious. This is the exclusion of subjectivity. How many subjects have been discarded and how many experiments spoiled because of a 'wrong' understanding on the part of the subject or because of his or her resistance to the experimental task? Experimental controls, when effective, serve their consciously intended purpose, which is to increase the passivity of subjects and to decrease their idiosyncrasies. It is precisely the subjectivity of the individual subject that is regarded as extraneous and must be controlled by being 'held constant'. But what about 'debriefing' and other post-experimental discussions with subjects about their experience of the task? These hardly constitute a recognition of the fundamental centrality of human subjectivity. They are more often used simply to assure the experimenter that the experimental controls have been effective.

We shall have more to say about experimental method later. What is clear already is that: (1) the method described above (or a reasonable facsimile) is applied nearly universally in academic psychology; (2) it is a method that follows directly from the behaviourist understanding of psychological subject matter as the correlation of input and output variables (subject as 'switchbox'); (3) it is a method directed at the isolation of the individual subject from his or her concrete life situation; and (4) it emphatically excludes the subjective element from anything but negative consideration.

There is, of course, nothing particularly new about this kind of analysis. There has probably never been a time in the historical existence of functional-behavioural experimental psychology when someone has not recognized the problem and made efforts to correct it. The rise of the 'third force' in the 1960s, consisting of humanistic, existential, and phenomenological psychologies, was but one dramatic instance of resistance to these essentially anti-human methods and the abstract knowledge that they produce. What is different in the present case is that the problem is not simply recognized, but accounted for in terms of the necessary reproduction by 'social' science, in both its theories and its methods, of the actual isolation and abstraction of individuals in the relations of bourgeois society. This will allow us to be critical, not just in the sense of objecting to something we know to be wrong but more positively by laying the groundwork for a more effective, subject-empowering psychology.

B.F. Skinner represents something of a paradox here. While he can rightly be taken as portraying the epitome of behaviourist thinking in twentieth-century psychology, he is also a critic of much of traditional psychological thinking and especially of traditional statistical method. It appears that his criticisms of standard method and his advocacy of individual analysis might be a corrective for the abstracting, isolating effects we are criticizing. Hopes are soon dashed, however, by the recognition that his argument is not with the isolation or the abstraction of the subject produced by standard methods, but with their lack of control. As Skinner put it in his 1953 book:

> [Our] argument is levelled at the use of statistics in a science of behavior. A prediction of what the *average* individual will do is often of little or no value in dealing with a particular individual. . . . In general, a science is helpful in dealing with the individual only insofar as its laws refer to individuals. . . . [A] science may also deal with the behavior of the individual, and its success in doing so must be evaluated in terms of its achievements rather than any a priori contentions.
>
> (Skinner 1953: 19)

It is obvious enough from this quotation that Skinner wants to be able to predict the behaviour of individuals in order to 'deal with' them. What does he mean by 'dealing with' them? As we read on, we learn that this is to 'shape and maintain behavior' (1953: 91ff). But can't we do that for ourselves as individuals? That may *appear* to be the case but ultimately 'society is responsible for the larger part of the behaviour of self-control. If this is correct, little ultimate control remains with the individual' (1953: 240). Pressing on, we learn that by 'society' Skinner appears to mean other people in general, other people in particular, or specific groups of other people.

There is nothing in Skinner's psychology to suggest that he has budged noticeably from Watson's definition of the aim of psychology as the prediction and control of individual behaviour. Most of the research that followed from Skinner's writings confirms this. The pioneering application of behaviour modification techniques to schizophrenic patients in a Saskatchewan hospital by Ayllon and Azrin (1963, 1964) proved very effective in 'dealing with' the patients. It did not alleviate their ailments, but it did 'improve their lives' by reducing friction between them and the hospital staff. In short, behaviour modification 'deals with' its subjects by adjusting them to the demands of the existing relations of authority.

Some more 'liberal' behaviour modifiers have recently come to emphasize people's use of behavioural techniques on themselves. This has the appearance of putting more control into the hands of concrete individuals, but closer examination reveals that it merely implicates them in establishing and maintaining their own conformity to existing relations.

A reading of *Walden Two* (Skinner 1948) makes all this clear enough, but there is nothing like a little first-hand experience. As a graduate student at the end of the 1950s I participated in a tour of the behavioural laboratory of a large institution for the mentally retarded. The chief researcher there had established a considerable reputation among his fellow Skinnerian behaviourists for work on schedules of reinforcement. Even then, in the innocence of my youth, I was startled to see that the laboratory consisted of a series of small, absolutely bare rooms, that is, bare except for a lever device on one wall and a small cup near it into which a candy reinforcer (the coated chocolate kind that 'don't melt in your hand') could be delivered. The assistant was quite proud of the levers which he had helped to adapt (ingeniously) from the squeezing levers of sponge mops discarded by the janitorial staff. The only thing beyond size that distinguished these rooms from the more familiar boxes used for rats and pigeons was a single, small chair on which the subject sat. Needless to say, the principal feature of the results from retarded children was their similarity to those produced by pigeons and rats.

Skinner himself, on more than one occasion, evinced great pride in this kind of generality, despite his avowed concern for the individual. A well-known example of this is found in a 1956 article in which he displays to the reader three cumulative curves side by side and unlabelled. In the text he writes that: 'one of them was made by a pigeon . . ., one was made by a rat . . ., and one was made by a monkey. . . . Pigeon, rat, monkey, which is which? It doesn't matter.' As long as one is able to 'deal with' the organism, it appears not to matter much what kind it is. How is such splendid generality achieved? There is only one answer: through isolation and abstraction of the subject. Is this the kind of knowledge (abstract knowledge), the kind of generality (abstract generality) that, say, gives individual subjects greater control over the conditions of their own lives? Not likely! If it empowers anyone, it is the one who 'deals with' the subjects and those in whose interests the 'dealing' is being done.

It is remarkable that when it came directly to the question of subjectivity, Skinner did not merely ignore it; he effectively 'theorized' it out of the way. When he did this, he did it in exactly the terms identified by the historical materialist analysis of the last chapter, namely, in terms of privacy. In his 1953 book he devoted an entire chapter to 'private events in a natural science'. He began the chapter as follows:

> When we say that behavior is a function of the environment, the term 'environment' presumably means any event in the universe capable of affecting the organism. But part of the universe is enclosed within the organism's own skin. . . . A private event may be distinguished by its limited accessibility but not, so far as we know, by any special structure or nature.
>
> (Skinner 1953: 257)

Skinner then proceeds to elaborate a theory of private events that asserts their essential similarity to public events. This means for him that both kinds of events are exhaustively understandable in terms of stimuli and conditioned behavioural responses. The only difference, as he mentioned, is accessibility. This creates a number of interesting problems. For example, when the child identifies a stove as hot the response can be confirmed and appropriately reinforced by experienced adults. When the child identifies some private event such as, say, a toothache, the adult is less able confidently to confirm or disconfirm this judgement. The result is that, as private individuals, we come to be surer (more reliable) in our public responses than in our private responses.

The consequent problematic nature of our private events and responses leads to a further theoretical-methodological result. This has to do with the question of the role played by private events in our public lives. The traditional view, according to Skinner, is that we act on the basis of some feeling or idea, i.e. some private event. There are two problems with this. First, the private event is both unreliable and inaccessible to the observer (the 'dealer') and thus serves as a poor basis for behavioural prediction and control. Second, whatever the reliability of the potentially reportable private event, it is

at best no more than a link in a causal chain, and it is usually not even that. We may think before we act in the sense that we may behave covertly before we behave overtly, but our action is not an 'expression' of the covert response or the consequence of it. The two are attributable to the same [external, public] variables.

(Skinner 1953: 279)

It follows from the point of view of prediction and control that the private event is superfluous and can be ignored. The only reliable predictor is the public stimulus. Subjectivity is thus an imperfect and unnecessary replicate or continuation of external events. Why unnecessary? Why imperfect? Because it is private! A rather neat disposal of a potentially troublesome issue.

It is fascinating that Skinner *seems* to have a theory of society from which he *seems* to *deduce* subjectivity. It does not require a very close examination, however, to see that society in his theory is nothing more than an ahistorical concatenation of isolated individuals, private parties, externally related to one another and in which the ideal state is one that is simply frictionless. He effectively started with an abstracted and isolated conception of the individual, created his theory of 'society' out of that, and then injected it back into the individual. The result is that both the theory and the deduction from it are shams, mere apparitions of the real theory of society and deductive procedure we are looking for.

The German Critical Psychologists have elaborated a critique of behaviourism that is far too detailed to consider here. Much of this is summarized in Holzkamp's recent book on learning (1993). The critique dates back to the first issue of *Forum Kritische Psychologie* in 1975 (*Kritische Psychologie [I]*), which was devoted to a discussion of behaviour therapy. Eva Jaeggi (1975) offered an apologetic defence of behaviour therapy on essentially utilitarian grounds. Irma Gleiss gave a critique of the sort that we have already articulated:

The independent and passive element in the relationship is the individual. By contrast, society is the active, moving element, independent of the individual. Consequently, society appears as the sum of external stimulus events that, although they provide contingencies for human behaviour, remain, however, foreign to it.

(Gleiss 1975: 60)

Wolfgang Maiers (1975) offered a still more detailed critique of behaviour therapy, stressing its ahistorical and non-societal basis.

COGNITIVE PSYCHOLOGY

If the so-called 'cognitive revolution' of the late 1960s had offered a genuine alternative to the previously dominant behavioural-functional psychology, we would require a separate critique of it here. But, in fact, it did not offer any such alternative, which reduces our task here to that of simply showing how it is really the same old wine in new bottles (even the bottles are sometimes the same; only the labels have been changed). Perhaps the most immediate and obvious clue to this is that cognitive psychologists continue to use the variable-model characteristic of behavioural-functional psychology with no essential modification beyond its further sophistication. This is important because the variable-model for method and theory is logically and necessarily linked to the anthropology of the abstract-isolated individual. Individuals are abstracted by their being represented as mere switchboxes for measured variables – or worse, by their being reduced to a mere assembly of such variables. They are isolated because this model fails to treat the relation between individuals and their societal, historical contexts as any different from any other collection of variables. The variable-model, as should already be clear from our previous discussion of it, is the very vehicle by which this anthropology is advanced and maintained.

Theories of cognitive psychology are also revealing. What we find is simply the variablized behavioural-functional, input–output model fitted out in more elaborate hypothetical constructs than traditionally allowed by the more self-consciously positivistic psychology.[1] Now instead of the more arid intervening variables like 'drive', 'reinforcement gradients', 'habit-family hierarchies', and 'fractional antedating goal-responses', we find complexly embellished metaphors such as 'information processing' and 'sentence analysing machinery'. The more primitive machines and 'flush toilet' hydraulic systems of behavioural-functional psychology have been replaced by the computer. The individual, however, is still abstracted and isolated.

The situation has not been greatly helped by the activity around social cognition that has given us theoretical concepts like 'attitude', 'attribution', and 'impression management' (see Gleitman 1991).[2] We are therefore not surprised to read in a recent critique of cognitive psychology by a cognitive psychologist that it has not saved us from the 'positivistic excesses of the behaviourists', as often claimed, but has carried many of these over into its own activity. Consequently:

> If the positivistic conception of science fails to capture many of the subtleties of collective epistemic practice in scientific communities, as is now generally acknowledged, then cognitivism must fail also as an approach to individual human cognition, and for the same reasons.
>
> (Smythe 1991: 103).

Cognitive psychologists have had little, if anything, to say about subjectivity. But the word 'consciousness' has become more frequently used. If we are correct in our assessment up to this point, however, we should not expect to find that cognitive psychology has brought us very far in our understanding of it. This seems to be confirmed by a recent comprehensive survey of the status of North American psychology by Ernest Hilgard:

> In the last quarter of the century the doors were open again [by virtue of the 'cognitive revolution'] to the study of consciousness in all of its manifestations, but there were no firmly established conceptions to return to, and a fully satisfactory modernization of scientific approaches to consciousness remained to be achieved.

> (Hilgard 1987: 315)

One of the striking features of recent cognitive psychology is the extent to which it has revived an experimental tradition that had great prominence in Wundt's experimental psychology laboratory at Leipzig, but which had effectively died out by the second or third decade of this century. I am speaking here of what was then called 'mental chronometry'. The technique was first developed by the Dutch physiologist Franciscus Donders in 1868, based on Helmholtz's experiments on the speed of nerve conduction (see Boring 1950: 148–149). It started with measurements of reaction time. Donders got the idea of complicating the experimental arrangement so as to require more work by the subject. For example, instead of being required to push a single button when a light went on, the subject was asked to push button 'a' if light 'A' went on, but button 'b' if light 'B' went on. Donders called this 'choice' as opposed to 'simple reaction'. Generally it took a little longer, so that the total time could be decomposed subtractively into a simple reaction component and a choice component. This produced what Donders considered to be 'mental constants' for each of the corresponding mental functions. Wundt went on to develop further complications to correspond with a long list of presumed mental functions like discrimination, cognition, association, and judgement.

The results of decades devoted to 'mental chronometry' were neatly summarized by Heidbreder:

> The idea was attractive, promising as it did the gratifying simplification that comes from reducing complex material to fixed, identifiable, quantitative units. But the subsequent analysis of reactions, simple and complex, gave little or no evidence of psychological 'constants'.

> (Heidbreder 1933: 89)

It is significant that Wundt himself insisted that the kind of experimental psychology represented by this practice could never yield theoretical understanding of the 'higher mental processes'. For this a more descriptive science of culture and history, a *Völkerpsychologie*, was needed.

What had died out by 1930 has been energetically revived by cognitive psychology, in which the dependent variable in experiments on presumably cognitive functioning is frequently, once again, some form of reaction time. One well-known example of this is an experiment by Shepard and Metzler (1971) in which subjects were shown two-dimensional drawings of two three-dimensional objects. The subject's task was to judge whether the two objects were identical or not. Where the objects were, in fact, identical they were represented in differing degrees of rotation. Successful subjects reported that they performed the required match by mentally rotating one of the figures to see if it conformed to the other. Reaction time was also measured and found to correlate with the actual degree of rotation portrayed in the pictures; that is, it took twice as long to make the judgement for figures that were rotated by 160 degrees as for figures rotated by only 80 degrees. It was these reaction times that were taken as confirmation of the introspective reports.

This is an undeniably attractive experiment. It is ingeniously conceived and the results are fascinating. It also yields some obviously important information about cognition, namely that the mind or brain has some kind of spatial processing capacity other than that which processes verbally coded meanings. Results like this, however, tell us virtually nothing about subjectivity, and certainly nothing about subjectivity as historically and societally situated. With a little more ingenuity, in fact, the experiment could have been done on rats or pigeons, who must also be pretty good at recognizing objects of importance to them from different angles, that is, in different rotations.

PSYCHOANALYSIS

From the point of view of our critique, psychoanalysis is a very complex position. It represents itself as an explicit theory of consciousness (via the unconscious) and subjectivity. For those interested in these topics it has captured, and continues to capture, the imagination in ways that distinguish it significantly from the prevailing behavioural-functional-cognitive psychologies. The mainstream academic response to psychoanalysis has been consistently hostile, maintaining that it is not really scientific and attracts only those sensitive to its literary or mystical qualities. This argument is difficult to sustain in face of historical reality. Psychoanalysis had its origin in the scientific physiology of the nineteenth century; it yields hypotheses that can be corroborated, that is, it is testable (see Flanagan 1984: 74–81); and it continues to have one of the best track records of all existing psychotherapies. It was scientific enough for the behaviourists John Dollard and Neal Miller to devote an entire book (1950) to making psychoanalysis accessible to other behaviourists – on their terms, of course.

The scientific character of psychoanalysis will not be questioned here. Instead, our discussion will have two objectives: (1) to show how, despite its other possible virtues, psychoanalysis still reproduces the hidden anthropology of which we have already spoken – that is, it is a bourgeois psychology, not a critical one – and its theory of subjectivity is therefore marked by serious distortions; and (2) to show how it is nevertheless exemplary as a science in ways that a Critical Psychology must emulate if it is to be successful.

We can move directly to the heart of our critique by turning to Freud's *Civilization and Its Discontents* (1930/1975). It is in this work that Freud's ideas about the relationship between the individual and society were most plainly laid out. His *The Future of an Illusion* (1927/1973) on the nature of religion had evoked a friendly response from Romain Rolland who expressed regret that Freud had still not really got to the heart of the issue, namely the source of the religious sentiment. Rolland made his own suggestion about this which Freud promptly dismissed, moving off immediately into his own speculations on the matter.

In a nutshell, Freud's account was this: religion exists as a consolation for human misery and suffering. What is the source of this suffering? It is civilization itself: '[W]hat we call our civilization is largely responsible for our misery, and . . . we should be much happier if we gave it up and returned to primitive conditions' (Freud 1930/1975: 23). Freud's analysis begins effectively with the individual who is, in his view, equipped biologically with two opposing instincts, Eros and death. The individual is driven into association with others to satisfy the sexual needs stemming from Eros and for protection against self-destruction, the latter being accomplished through redirection of aggression towards others. The 'evolution of civilization', according to Freud, is nothing but the 'struggle between Eros and Death, between the instinct of life and the instinct of destruction, as it works itself out in the human species' (1930/1975: 59). Near the end of the book the point is further elaborated:

> [T]he two urges, the one towards personal happiness and the other towards union with other human beings, must struggle with each other in every individual; and so, also, the two processes of individual and of cultural development must stand in hostile opposition to each other and mutually dispute the ground. But this struggle between the individual and society is not a derivative of the contradiction – probably an irreconcilable one – between the primal instincts of Eros and death. It is a dispute within the economics of the libido, comparable to the contest concerning the distribution of libido between ego and objects; and it does admit of an eventual accommodation in the individual, as, it may be hoped, it will also do in the future of civilization, however much that civilization may oppress the life of the individual today.
>
> (Freud 1930/1975: 78)

This may be the most optimistic view expressed in the entire book but it also reveals the nature of Freud's analysis. It is not a great deal different from Skinner's. It begins with some assumptions about the nature of the individual psyche, creates from those assumptions a theory of society, which it then introjects back into the individual. It is a richer and more interesting account than Skinner's, but it has the same character. The end result is a picture of the individual abstracted from society, fundamentally isolated, and finally forced into essentially external relations with others, a reproduction of the Hobbesian 'war of all against all', which in Freud's treatment comes out as an explicit 'war of each against society' (Skinner being somewhat more optimistic about the eventual reduction of friction). The hidden anthropology of bourgeois thought is thus once again laid bare.

Freud himself makes clear the connection between these ideas and the bourgeois form of societal existence. He explicitly objects to the socialist proposal to abolish private property in the means of production. Of course, he does this not on political grounds, but on ostensibly scientific-psychological ones:

> [T]he psychological premises on which the system [socialism or communism] is based are an untenable illusion. In abolishing private property we deprive the human love of aggression of one of its instruments, certainly a strong one, though certainly not the strongest; but we have in no way altered the differences in power and influence which are misused by aggressiveness, nor have we altered anything in its nature.
>
> (Freud 1930/1975: 50)

No, the injustices in the system should be left alone because they are natural: '[N]ature, by endowing individuals with extremely unequal physical attributes and mental capacities, has introduced injustices against which there is no remedy' (1930/1975: 50fn). Indeed, Freud suggests that to meddle in this natural, though admittedly miserable, state of affairs is likely only to create something much worse. *Laissez-faire*!

It should surprise no one, then, that Marxists have been critical of Freud (for a more detailed, specifically critical-psychological critique see Holzkamp-Osterkamp 1976). But the relationship between Marxism and Freudism has not been quite as simple as this suggests. In fact, there has been a continuing debate within Marxist circles over the relationship since early in this century and extending with full vigour to our own time. In the context of Critical Psychology, Holzkamp made an interesting and insightful contribution to this debate in 1984 (English trans. 1991b). He began by admitting his acceptance of the standard Marxist critique of Freud that 'psychoanalysis essentially biologizes and individualizes its subject matter, that it psychologizes social conflicts, postulates a universal opposition between the repressing society and the unsocial drive-determined individual, abets irrationalism, and so forth' (1991b: 81). He went on to point out how the Critical Psychologists had stood in constant opposition not only to Freudians, but to Freudo-Marxists (cf. Braun 1979).

Holzkamp's credentials as an opponent of psychoanalysis are well established. There remain in his view, however, two important questions that need to be addressed. First, if psychoanalysis has been so conclusively and devastatingly criticized by progressively inclined people, Marxists and non-Marxists alike, why are we still debating it? Why is it not dead and buried like the theory of phlogiston in the physical sciences or phrenology in psychology? What is it about psychoanalysis that makes it so hardy?

Second, why, as it continues its mysterious existence, is it precisely people on the progressive political left who continue to be so attracted to it? Why the constant revivals of Wilhelm Reich? Why the vast array of more recent Freudo-Marxisms? There are no other psychologists who have attracted attention from the political left: one hears nothing of Skinnero-Marxists, Hullo-Marxists, or even Maslowio-Marxists (and Maslow was a self-proclaimed socialist)!

Considerations like these arouse a related and still more general question about Freud's wide appeal to scholars and scientists outside psychology, as in literary studies, art, linguistics, religious studies, ethnology, and sociology. Again, no equivalent interest can be found for any other psychologist of the twentieth century. Holzkamp feels himself forced to the initial conclusion that, when all the obvious weaknesses and deficiencies of psychoanalysis are taken into account, there remains something of profound value that needs to be identified.

Holzkamp begins by noting a significant difference between the modern behavioural-functional approach to consciousness and that of classical (nineteenth-century) German psychology. While consciousness and subjectivity became troublesome for mainstream twentieth-century psychologists because of their emphasis on prediction and control, the classical psychologists were less utilitarian and understood consciousness as a mediator of the individual's relations with the world and with other people. It was thus something to be understood in its own right. Consciousness was not thought of as exclusively private, but as a kind of intersubjectivity that, like meaning, was shared as a collective cultural product. This was the conception of consciousness that was addressed by Wundt's *Völkerpsychologie*, and which he felt could not be touched by experimental psychology. Other German thinkers of the late nineteenth century shared this view: Franz Brentano and Wilhelm Dilthey were but two of these. By Holzkamp's assessment Freud also belonged to this group. 'If we want to do justice to psychoanalysis . . . we must place it directly in the developmental line of classical [German] psychology' (1991b: 91).

The object of investigation for Freud, as for the other German psychologists, was immediate experience. Freud understood his task as the 'objective clarification and investigation of this experience as subjective–intersubjective relation to self and the world' (Holzkamp 1991b: 91). For Freud especially, the immediate experience that required attention was that 'in which lies concealed the socially repressive relations as they are felt in people's concrete life circumstances' (Holzkamp 1991b: 91).

In order to support the study of subjectivity, Freud developed a categorial system aimed at elucidating the subjective situation of his subjects rather than at predicting and controlling their behaviour. His assumption was that, if his subjects or patients understood their subjective situations, they would be able to choose for themselves appropriate courses of action. For example, concepts like 'ego, id, and superego were intended as a means of dramatizing the contradictory tendencies and impulses of immediate experience in order to deal with them more consciously, that is, to bring them under control' (Holzkamp 1991b: 92). What might count here as 'dealing with' and 'control' are, in contrast to behavioural-functional psychology, dealing and controlling by the subject. In short, the intention of the analysis and the categorial or conceptual system was to empower the subject, not the psychoanalyst or those he or she may have represented.

Translation of these categories into behavioural-functionalist terms, such as was done by Dollard and Miller (1950), utterly violates their intended function (cf. Holzkamp 1985). Holzkamp cites the example of repression, which in the psychoanalytic context is intended as an aid to the subject in identifying and thereby overcoming infantile impulses that are interfering with the subject's own dealing with present conflicts. When this concept is operationalized into a shift from a later learned response to an earlier one while under stress, it is certainly more accessible to empirical and experimental testing (it can even be tested on rats), but 'this takes the concept out of the subjective–intersubjective experiential context and thus . . . totally robs it of its meaning and function' (Holzkamp 1991b: 92).

The 'Oedipus complex' provides a particularly revealing example of the empowering nature of Freud's theory. It is wrong, Holzkamp claims, to think of this complex as something restricted to a set of empirical events within a family constellation. This would be to miss Freud's point that the particular empirical events found in middle-class Viennese families were merely expressions of the more general social dynamic resulting in the 'inexorable and irrevocable suppression of the possibilities for [individual] satisfaction and fulfilment by an overpowering and punitive authority' (Holzkamp 1991b: 93), which is characteristic of bourgeois society. Any particular empirical instance of suppression is a manifestation of the more fundamental societal dynamic, which is not revealed in all its particulars by the empirical events, but must be discovered through special analytic efforts. As Marx remarked in the third volume of *Capital*: 'All science would be superfluous, if the appearance, the form, and the nature of things were wholly identical' (Marx 1894/1909: 951). Freud was attempting to reveal – that is, to make objective – the underlying nature of the problem so as to help the individual to elucidate his or her own subjective experience, and thereby also to acquire the means by which to deal with his or her own unhappiness.

Freud's analysis of the underlying dynamic also yielded the category of the 'superego'. It was intended to show how the individual became an agent of his or her own suppression through the internalization of external authority.

> The superego concept thus had the function of making it possible [for the individual] to penetrate the subjectively given appearance of conscience, with the related guilt feelings, and to see the societally repressive relations that are hidden in it.
>
> (Holzkamp 1991b: 94)

On the one hand, we see Freud's view of society as the enemy. On the other, we discover a critical insight into the societal nature of the individual personality, which is not apparent in Freud's explicit treatments of the relationship between individual and society such as are found in *Civilization and Its Discontents*. From the modern critical point of view the error in Freud's overall analysis was the standard bourgeois one of taking the oppressive dynamic as given for the nature of society, rather than as a particular expression of the historical form of bourgeois society (a point also missed by the anthropologist Margaret Mead when she undertook to test the 'Oedipal complex hypothesis' in Samoan society in 1928).

The function that the psychological categories fulfil here is to mediate between the subjective experience of the individual and objective societal relations. This is very different from the nature of the categories found in behavioural-functional psychology. The difference becomes clearest in connection with claims about their *generality*. In behavioural-functional psychology a concept is considered general as it approaches universality, that is, when it is representative of all cases. Thus reinforcement is thought to be a general concept because it can allegedly be found in all cases of behavioural modification. The history of this concept reveals, however, that in order to achieve its generality it must become increasingly rarefied – indeed, rarefied to the point where it can only be defined as 'anything contingent upon a response that increases the probability of that response's future occurrence'. A definition like this achieves its generality through such a high degree of abstraction that it becomes impossible to identify a reinforcer before the fact, and thus renders the definition circular and non-falsifiable. Such statistical-empirical-universal generality is not what Freud was seeking.

Again in accord with much of nineteenth-century German philosophy and science (cf. Lewin 1931), Freud accepted the view that 'a theoretical conception of the structural and organizational principles of the psyche is general if by demonstrating the immanent objective structure of immediate experience it makes that experience comprehensible as intersubjectively homogeneous and accessible' (Holzkamp 1991b: 94). Empirical uniformity is not the goal of this kind of generality: 'differences in personal experience are not eliminated through recourse to extraneous factors but rather are elucidated by the mediational processes and levels that are part and parcel of the theory' (1991b: 95). The criterion for generality is, in short, not empirical universality but the capacity to elucidate the individual, often seemingly deviant, case. Individual differences are not thereby relegated to error variance.

This is the positive side of Critical Psychology's critique of psychoanalysis. It reveals both the basis for its continuing appeal to politically progressive people and that which in psychoanalysis must be emulated by a truly Critical Psychology that hopes to shed light on individual subjectivity in bourgeois society.

THE PROBLEM OF THEORETICAL INDETERMINACY

In a paper published in 1977 and reprinted in 1978 (which is the version to which I shall be referring), Klaus Holzkamp addressed the problem of the indeterminacy of psychological theories, a problem that was becoming the focus of the debates of that decade on the 'crisis in social psychology' (e.g. Arnold 1976;

Elms 1975), and which subsequently became more generally formulated as psychology's 'crisis of disunity' (e.g. Staats 1983; cf. Maiers 1987). Although in his paper Holzkamp identified the problem, diagnosed its causes, and outlined its solution within the context of Critical Psychology, we shall here be concerned mainly with identification and diagnosis, postponing the solution to the final chapter of the book.

Serge Moscovici, an early contributor to the 'crisis' literature in social psychology, deplored the acceptance by his colleagues of common sense over theory, the proliferation of experimental studies lacking theoretical preoccupations, and the isolation of one area of research from another. The accumulated facts that result, he noted, 'do not amount to real progress', and 'no theory is, in any real sense, disconfirmed or replaced by another'. The end result was that 'the empirically established facts are nothing but a heterogeneous collection, as are the theories on which they are supposed to depend' (Moscovici 1972: 43–44).

Charles Catania observed that while students were being asked to 'choose theoretical sides' from among a bewildering array of competing points of view, 'psychologists [themselves] are not yet even agreed on whether theirs is a science of behaviour or science of mental life' (Catania 1973: 434).

Outside of social psychology the problem was recognized already in 1966 by Ernest Hilgard and Gordon Bower. They expressed perplexity over the apparent lack of cumulative gain from the massive amounts of research results produced in psychological laboratories. It seemed self-evident to them that 'the more we know the more we should be able to find out, but the history of our science does not bear this out' (Hilgard and Bower 1966: 582). Research problems, they note, are often abandoned before they are solved. The 'thoughtful systematic approaches' needed in order to see questions through to their answers appeared to be lacking in psychology. Hilgard and Bower's recommendation was that 'some good high-level thinking is needed, keeping in mind *criteria of relevancy*, so that significant controversies are resolved on the basis of firmer knowledge' (1966: 583).

Back in social psychology, a somewhat more diagnostic view of the situation was expressed by Rom Harré and Paul Secord:

The need for a comprehensive theoretical treatment of social psychology and for a reformed methodology we feel to be pressing, and to be evident from the increasing dissatisfaction with the state of social psychology, even within the citadels of the profession. The underlying reason for this state we believe to be a continued adherence to a positivist methodology, long after the theoretical justification for it, in naive behaviourism, has been repudiated. At present there is scarcely any coherent body of theory. In such a vacuum it is still possible to carry on empirical studies which make sense only if people are conceived of in the mechanical tradition as passive entities whose behaviour is the product of 'impressed forces', and whose own contribution to social action is the latent product of earlier impressed experience. A methodology of experiment survives in which the typical investigation is recommended to be a manipulation of 'variables', and the typical result a correlation in the manner of Boyle's Law.

(Harré and Secord 1972: 1)

These are sentiments that resonate clearly with the Critical Psychologists' call for criteria for relevance and their deploring of the variable-model, together with its implications for theory and method.

Holzkamp (1977; see also Tolman 1988, 1989b, 1991b) believes we can detect the nature of the problem by examining our normal practice. Starting with a typical psychological theory in mind (it hardly matters which one, or from what area of psychology), we deduce hypotheses, which are then translated into the language of independent and dependent variables. Experimental design and statistical assessment are used to ensure both necessity and sufficiency of the independent variable conditions with regard to the expected result. If the result occurs and is judged reliable, the hypothesis and theory are treated as having been confirmed.

In this procedure there are two sources of theoretical indeterminacy, one minor and one major. The minor one is what might be called 'weak confirmation'. Our experimental and statistical methods have come to be so highly refined that under existing rules of procedure almost any selected relationship has very favourable chances of being confirmed. Holzkamp has called this *Bestätigungsfreundlichkeit* (literally, confirmation-friendliness). He shows how this is supported by our standard criteria for null hypothesis testing. With the right sample size and 'alpha level', it takes very little explained variance to count as a confirmation of the experimental hypothesis (that is, speaking more strictly, to reject the null hypothesis).

Holzkamp is not suggesting that this is wrong in itself. Nor is he saying that these methods should be relaxed or abandoned entirely. That would surely only make matters worse. Rather, he is pointing out how our methods allow the confirmation of hypotheses, which, though correct, may be utterly *irrelevant* or *non-essential*.

The major source of theoretical indeterminacy is a lack of broader perspective. While we may go on confirming our theory *ad infinitum*, we may never learn from our efforts whether the particular hypothesis or theory is actually relevant or essential to the understanding of psychological process. Another theorist, interpreting the particular process in other, even opposing, terms, and adopting similar experimental procedures, may likewise find infinite confirmations. The resolution of the differences between the theories is therefore not to be sought in further empirical confirmation or further refinement of experimental methods. What is missing is the broader perspective from which relevance and essentiality can be judged.

What does Holzkamp mean, then, by *relevant*, and *essential*? In his work on 'theoretical indeterminacy', Holzkamp refers to relevance as

a *real* mark of status within the dimensional structure, such that theories become scientifically more relevant, i.e. capable of carrying more real knowledge, to the extent that they conceptually embrace more relevant dimensions: dimensions are . . . more *essential* than others to the extent that they are more *fundamental*, i.e. depend less on others than others on them, and consequently a variety of different superficial phenomena, the variability of which derives from less essential dimensions, are lawfully related to one another by virtue of relation to them.

(Holzkamp 1978: 157)

How is essentiality determined? From an evolutionary point of view, essential is what contributes to survival. It is essential that an organism respond appropriately to the demands placed upon it by its environmental context. Essentiality of a process can thus be determined by a study of the evolutionary or other developmental processes and contexts that have shaped it.

This is admittedly not an entirely satisfactory answer but it is only intended at this point to indicate a general direction for further development. The idea is that, if we know how a process has evolved or developed, we can discover what is relevant and essential to it. And if we can develop non-arbitrary criteria for relevance and essentiality, it should be possible to be guided by them in the formulation of our theories and hypotheses in such a way as to provide a basis for a general, integrative ordering of our knowledge of psychological processes. That is the task that Critical Psychology undertakes in its reconstruction of psychology, and it will come as no surprise to learn that the positive insights gained in our critique of psychoanalysis will play an important role.

Part III

Reconstruction

Chapter 5

Reconstructing the psychological categories

Traditional psychology rests on a set of basic categories that are seldom questioned. They form the major headings in all our introductory texts: learning, motivation, memory, emotion, personality, development, sensation, perception, etc. We sometimes acknowledge problems in defining them but don't normally allow ourselves to become preoccupied with those problems. The norm in this century has been to seek procedural rules by which definitions can be fixed and agreed upon so that we can 'get on with the business' of doing psychology. Perhaps the best known means of achieving such expediency have been provided by the operational definition. When we undertake an investigation of, say, learning or perception, we generally accept the definitions given by the current textbooks and experimental literature – indeed, we know very well we won't get published if we don't!

Critical Psychologists believe that the basic category system, together with its seemingly authoritative definitions, cannot and should not be taken for granted. The reason for this will already be clear from the sketch of their critique in the preceding chapters. Taking the categories and their definitions for granted runs the risk of reproducing in our science the ideologically saturated understandings of everyday existence in bourgeois society. It is through the categories of bourgeois psychology that the concealed anthropology of the isolated individual continues to dominate our thinking. For example, for most of this century learning was treated as the central category of psychology. It was defined in terms of stimulus–response connections that could be weakened or strengthened by external contingencies called reinforcers. It requires little effort to see that this represents a reproduction in psychological theory of the prevailing relations of production in which the activity of workers is controlled through wages and in which every worker is considered a 'free agent' in a system of independent individuals looking out for themselves by selling their labour at the going rate. A conception of learning like this is anything but 'value-neutral'.

Learning does occur, however, and it is important in our real, everyday lives. Critical Psychologists do not deny this, nor do they deny that the bourgeois conception of learning represents real events and is thus true in the narrowest sense. The problem is not so much that bourgeois theories are false (though they may indeed be that), as that they take their partial truths as a fully adequate description of our societal reality and of our lives in that reality. This must be the target of our critique. Moreover, it is not our intent to replace the behaviourist's conception of truth *in* bourgeois relations with some alternative conception that itself remains *in* bourgeois relations: it is to develop a Critical Psychology that is *about* individuals acting and experiencing in bourgeois relations. This means, as we have already seen, stepping outside the strictly psychological framework to see that psychology is part of a larger understanding of historical, societal human existence, and this requires a careful re-examination of our basic categories of thought with a view to reconstructing them critically in order to achieve the transition from *in* to *about*.

The account of Critical Psychology's categorial reconstruction that follows is based on Klaus Holzkamp's book *Grundlegung der Psychologie* (1983).[1] The German word *Grundlegung* does not have a ready English equivalent but suggests a rebuilding from the ground up. In the book's densely composed 600 pages Holzkamp undertakes, among other things, a thorough reconstruction of psychology's categorial system. We will obviously be able only to scratch the surface of this monumental effort here. In this chapter I will try to indicate how Holzkamp approached the problem of reconstruction and to outline the essential details of his method. I hope that it will become evident how the new category system develops to the point that enables us to understand some of its major implications for specifically human psychological functioning, which will then be elaborated in the chapters that follow.

It will be useful to remind ourselves of a methodological point already alluded to, namely that our categories, especially as they pertain to individual human subjectivity, must not be defined independently of a theory of society and then afterward merely attached to such a theory. The general methodological principle is one of deduction (though, again, not in the formal logical, but logical-historical sense). We must be able to show the *necessity* of the interrelations between the biological, societal, and individual subjective aspects of our being. Holzkamp will seek a 'most fundamental' category, elaborate it, and then attempt to deduce further categories from it, arriving finally at the conscious subjective state familiar to us as adult human beings.[2]

'PSYCHE' AS THE MOST FUNDAMENTAL CATEGORY[3]

When it comes to questions of psychological functioning there can be nothing more basic than life itself. Surely it is a reasonable assumption that what we call psyche or psychical process represents a qualitatively distinct outgrowth from more general life-processes. What is the general life-process? It is what essentially distinguishes dandelions, amoebas, baboons, and humans from rocks and other purely 'physical' objects or substances. There are some important differences here that we will need to be aware of. For one thing, when a physical substance is once formed it does not depend on interaction with other physical substances for its preservation. A rock left entirely alone will remain a rock. When physical things are brought into interaction, either or both of two kinds of result may occur. Quantitatively, their motions may change, as in direction or speed, without themselves being essentially changed, or they may change in size and number, as a rock when it is broken. If, however, the interaction should affect the thing's quality, that is, its 'essential nature', the result will be the destruction of the initial nature and its replacement by another. This is what happens in a chemical reaction. For example, when zinc and sulphuric acid come into interaction, both are significantly changed in their qualitative natures, the outcome being zinc sulphate and hydrogen.

In short, ordinary physico-chemical substances tend to be destroyed or qualitatively transformed by interaction. They do not *require* interaction in order to preserve their qualitative distinctness; indeed for this they require the absence of interaction. The most obvious feature of living substances, by contrast, is that they *do* require interaction in order to preserve themselves, and ultimately to reproduce themselves. When a living substance interacts with another substance – whether living or not is irrelevant here – the normal result is the destructive transformation of the other substance *as required* for the preservation of the first; that is, the first, living substance continues to exist, preserves its essential quality, by *metabolizing* other substances.

What happens to the energy generated by the interaction also serves to distinguish living from non-living substances. In the case of the latter, energy is lost or dissipated (the standard example of entropy). In the case of living substances, however, energy is absorbed, stored, and used later for self-maintenance and reproduction.

Metabolism characterizes both the intraorganismic processes and the organism's relations with its environment. It is an *active* process, so that at the level, say, of the individual organism we can say that the organism must be active with respect to those substances required for its survival. The amoeba, for example, must actively embrace and absorb the objects it requires for its own metabolic processes. This kind of activity is said to reflect the *irritability* of living substance.

Thus far, the organism with its metabolizing, irritable, self-organizing capacities is still 'prepsychical'. It represents all the essential qualities associated with life. A central feature here is self-reproduction achieved through the passage of DNA and other organizing substances from one generation to the next. This feature, as we know, is subject to change in response to demands placed on the organism by its environment. The result is evolutionary change that generally increases the organism's capacity to exploit its environment for purposes of survival and reproduction.

Two developments at this prepsychical stage prepare the way for the evolutionary emergence of distinctly psychical processes. On the one hand, we can assume that evolutionary pressures are operating that will increase the organism's range of irritability, that is, it will become increasingly able to exploit its environment by developing irritability to a greater range of environmental properties. On the other hand, we can expect increasing pressures for the organism to locomote. The capacity for locomotion may develop in the first place as a means of ingesting foreign objects, as exemplified by the pseudopodia of the amoeba or the flagella of certain protozoa. Pressures to develop means of locomotion come first from the resulting increase in probability that the organism comes into contact with the substances it requires. This, in turn, makes it possible for the organism to exploit environments that are more and more heterogeneous, which, in turn, will further increase pressure on locomotion.

The prepsychical organism that is prepared for the qualitative transition to functioning at the most basic psychical level, then, is one that is irritable to a wide range of environmental properties, some of which may have only indirect bearing on their survival owing to association with more vital properties; is mobile, although mainly in a still random, 'kinetic' way; and has moved into a relatively heterogeneous (liquid) environment that is not evenly hospitable. Transition to the psychical level of functioning occurs when the evolutionary process brings all this together to yield an organism that can begin to locomote in an oriented fashion, responding to properties it cannot metabolize or that are not otherwise directly essential to its survival (such as light in many instances) in order to locate the substances that are essential to its survival. On the organism's side, Holzkamp, following Leontyev, calls this new capacity *sensibility*. The transition involved here marks a significant nodal point in evolutionary development. The qualities of the primitive psyche are deducible (in our special developmental sense) from the qualities of merely vital existence, that is, existed in them as a possibility, but, once realized, created possibilities that did not previously exist. It is the further development of these possibilities that marks the subsequent, progressive evolution of the psyche, which ultimately reaches the point of individual human consciousness and subjectivity.

THE FUNCTIONAL-HISTORICAL METHOD

The procedure by which Holzkamp, elaborating on the earlier analysis by Leontyev, works out the transition from the prepsychical to the psychical, thus identifying and defining the most fundamental category of psychical functioning, is called the 'functional-historical' method.[4] It is not a purely formal-logical method but relies heavily on the empirical evidence of other sciences such as physics, chemistry, biology, and paleontology. The deduction upon which it focuses passes through five identifiable steps.

The first step is to identify the historically relevant features of the stage preceding the development of the level of functioning of interest (and its related category). In a sense, this means finding out where the evolutionary action is. In the example already given this location was defined by a convergence of a number of features having to do with the organism's capability of preserving itself, that is, fulfilling its vital capacity, through differentiation of its irritability, development of mobility, and its extension to heterogeneous environments. One might say that this step of the analysis is concerned with finding the objective premises that will, in the evolutionary-developmental sense, yield the new category as their conclusion.

The second step is to identify the evolutionary forces at work at the earlier stage. This means focusing on the environmental pressures that are forcing changes in the organism through mutation or other evolutionary processes. From a dialectical point of view this can be expressed as identifying the contradictions developing between the organism's internal processes and the demands of the environment that will ultimately lead to qualitative change in the organism's mode of functioning. In our example, the heterogeneity of the environmental medium is a key factor in this regard.

The third step is to identify the crucial 'shift of function' (*Funktionswechsel*) in the elements revealed in the first step. In the present example the increase in range of properties to which the organism is irritable, the development of mobility, and the integration of these two elements yield a shift in the function served by certain properties in the organism's environment. The function of an environmental property as a simple attractant because it is required by the organism for survival changes into the function of a purely orientational 'signal'. In other words, the organism now detects and responds to a particular property not because it is what the organism needs or can metabolize, but because it serves to locate such substances. A common example would be that of simple organisms responding to light (either positively or negatively) because the food they require is more likely to be found in either the light or the dark.

The fourth step is the identification of the 'shift of dominance' (*Dominanzwechsel*) of the old and new functions. The overall evolutionary transition from the old to the new stage of development will undoubtedly be a long and continuous one, but at some point there will be a shift from an organism that has merely become capable of utilizing properties as signals to an organism that is characterized by both its capacity for use of signals and its dependence on signals. With regard to dependence, one can imagine that as the ability to exploit more complex environments develops, the organism comes increasingly to inhabit such environments, environments in which it now can only survive if the corresponding abilities continue to evolve. There is a point, in short, at which the organism 'can't go home again': its whole mode of existence is now qualitatively different.

The fifth step is the precise identification of the systemic nature of this qualitative difference. The shifts in function and then in dominance will necessarily have impacts upon other aspects of the organism's existence such that the evolutionary change can only be fully characterized (categorially defined) as a restructuring of the overall system. This, in turn, will create new possibilities and pressures for further development, thus returning at a higher level to step one of the method. The identification of these new possibilities is an important part of the investigation at this step.

Having defined the most fundamental category, psyche (with its principal characteristic of sensibility), and at the same time also having specified the outlines of the functional-historical method, the method can then be applied to working out the subsequent differentiation of the psyche. The major results of such an analysis will be summarized in the following sections. Four general areas of prehominid development will be outlined: (1) orientation and meaning; (2) emotionality and need; (3) communication and social structures; and (4) modifiability, learning, and individual development. The first three will be seen to be the further development of possibilities created by the first major transformation from the prepsychical to the psychical. They effectively become the conditions for developments in the fourth, which will finally constitute a second major evolutionary transformation.

ORIENTATION AND MEANING STRUCTURES

The evolutionary advantages gained for the organism by the mobility and sensibility that characterize the most primitive psychical level of development are not, strictly speaking, advantages for the individual organism but for the population of organisms. As we shall see, the individual organism only emerges as an evolutionary entity at a later, much more complex level of development. Seeing the problem, at least initially, as one of populations, which was one of Darwin's most notable insights, allows us to account for a number of important things. Among these is that the advantages we are concerned with are always *statistical* in nature: they work because they increase the population's adaptability *on the average*. A corollary of this is that individual organisms within a population may display a wide range of ability when it comes to, say, mobility and the use of environmental properties as signals. It is, of course (again, one of Darwin's important insights), precisely this variability within populations that permits the selection that shapes new capacities. To understand the significance of 'population thinking' in our theorizing about less evolved species will also help us later to appreciate more clearly its inappropriateness at the human level. What we must be prepared to see in the remainder of this chapter is that one of the major thrusts of evolutionary development is precisely the emergence of the individual organism as an evolutionarily significant unit.

Prior to the emergence of sensibility, mobility was characterized by 'kinesis', that is, essentially undirected or random movement. At some point appropriate conditions gave rise to the possibility, and then the actuality, of taxic or directed movement. The most primitive form of taxic movement was related to stimulus *gradients*. These were essentially gradients of density of energy (such as light) in which organisms tended to move so as to increase or to decrease their intensity. The organisms thus used the gradients as 'information', and its relevance to the organisms' activity can be spoken of as the most primitive form of 'meaning'. This does not imply in the least that they had any 'consciousness' or 'experience' of light's meaning, only that they moved towards or away as was adaptively appropriate. The orientation and the execution of movements were effectively identical. With the emergence of taxic orientation and, again, given the appropriate environmental pressures, it became possible for certain stimulus properties to function exclusively as signals of other stimulus properties.

Out of this orientation to gradients arose the capacity to *select* among environmental properties, which is a qualitatively new kind of information usage. At this stage organisms are able to *identify* conditions, which means responding to invariances in the environmental flux. Only with such a capacity, for instance, could they develop the ability to detect conditions at a distance and thus more truly *orient* themselves in space, as opposed to merely responding to that with which they were immediately in contact. At this stage orientation becomes a function for itself, relatively independent of the execution of movement.

There follows the development of the capacity for *discrimination* among differing units of objective meaning. This implies not merely the segregating of a particular unit out from an otherwise undifferentiated environment but the ability to respond to the difference between one unit and another, that is, the ability to respond to *relations* among units. At this point the organisms are not merely reacting to their environment by moving towards or away from something, but are able to respond to stimulus patterns with more differentiated behaviour. Again, however, we must keep in mind that while the animals are responding to relations, the relations need not exist as such for the animals as they do consciously for humans. Likewise, we need not assume that the relations between stimulus patterns and responses are mediated by anything but the organism's physiological state. For the animal the stimulus pattern for a predator is effectively identical with fleeing or crouching or whatever its protective response may be.

One of the interesting developments noted by Holzkamp (1983: 93–95) in connection with the evolution of orientational and meaning capacities is the eventual necessity for the development of individual priorities. Reproduction is primarily concerned with populations, because it is essentially populations that reproduce. In the most primitive organisms the pressures will favour the development of orientational and meaning processes that promote reproduction of the population. As the organisms and the environments they utilize become more complex, however, individual survival becomes increasingly significant in mediating the reproduction of the population. Thus orientational mechanisms and meaning structures begin to develop that pertain to the survival of individuals. Meaning units (such as stimulus complexes) increasingly assume individual, in addition to population, relevance. This, in turn, lays an important foundation for the development of individual learning and development, which will be discussed in the last section of this chapter.

EMOTIONALITY AND NEED STRUCTURES

The life activity of organisms already at the prepsychic level is dependent on their internal conditions, if only on the metabolic imbalances that lead to ingestion or egestion. And the developments in orientation and meaning structures already discussed presuppose corresponding changes in the roles these internal states play in the lives of the animals. It should be clear, for example, that a taxic response to, say, a light gradient cannot be the *immediate* result of the light itself. At the very least it presupposes an activating state of imbalance in the organism's physiology as a mediator. Meanings, therefore, must be considered as both actual and potential. At the psychical level a connection develops between particular alterations in organismic state and the actualization of particular meanings through the conversion of the state into action. This represents a *functional shift* of state variability from merely an expression of metabolic imbalances to the basis for the actualization of meanings. Considering that such conversions are always concerned with the maintenance of systemic balance, it is possible to speak of the related actualizations of meanings as *assessments* of the environmental conditions and of their appropriateness to the state of imbalance of the system. The standard for assessment, then, becomes the variable state of the organism. Putting it more loosely but more familiarly, the organism uses its own state as a measure of the appropriateness of a particular action in a given environment.

This sort of assessment becomes increasingly evident as the orientational capacities become more differentiated. In complex environments and with complex response possibilities, the organism may be forced to 'choose'. It can do this (though not consciously) on the basis of the assessment standard provided by its own state. Moreover, in such situations the activating internal states attain the status of signs with negative valence, while the external meaning units, through their actualization, attain the status of signs with positive valence. The degree of positivity or negativity of these valences will reflect the internal standard.

Holzkamp's categorial definition of emotionality follows from these considerations:

> Emotionality is the assessment of the environmental information received in the process of orientation, that is 'cognitively', against the standard of the momentary state of the organism or individual, and thus of the degree and mode of its preparedness for action.
>
> (Holzkamp 1983: 98)

According to this understanding, actions never follow directly from 'cognitions' or, in the earliest stages, from 'information received' but only through the qualitative assessment of the information, that is, through emotion. Considering its origin in the orientational necessities related to survival, emotion is thus seen as an objective representation within the organism of environmental conditions in terms of their survival value.

Since emotional assessments are actualizations of meanings, the evolutionary differentiation of the emotional dimension is closely connected to differentiation of the meaning dimension. Holzkamp refers to the actual differentiations themselves as 'need dimensions' (*Bedarfsdimensionen*). Need dimensions, of which more will need to be said, are distinguished from particular needs or need states. That is, we can speak of an animal's capacities for hunger or thirst as need dimensions without concerning ourselves with the particular ways in which these needs are manifested physiologically or behaviourally in any particular animal.

Given what has been said about need dimensions, etc., we note that organisms at the prepsychical level have these too. They have tissue deficits related to metabolic needs having to do with nutrition, fluid balance, temperature, etc., which would appear to count as need dimensions. Indeed, these are the fundamental need dimensions of traditional bourgeois psychology. But there is a problem here. If we are to take these as basic need dimensions and attempt to elaborate an account of complex human needs based on them, as traditional Hullian and Skinnerian learning theories do, we will be overlooking the most important point that we have made here: that such need dimensions are pre-psychical. Does something happen to such needs with the emergence of the psychical stage of development? What marks this stage off from its predecessor is the use by organisms – whether populations or individuals, but increasingly the latter – of non-metabolizable irritants as orientational signals (such as the light mentioned below). When this happens, the organism's biological existence itself achieves a new quality in that it begins to function in relative independence of its immediate metabolic needs. The need dimensions of animals at the psychical level, therefore, should be expected to display relations to their environments that are not governed immediately by strictly metabolic needs. This then applies to all the orientational and emotional developments that we have discussed.

The evidence of this grows as the organism becomes evolutionally more complex. How else, for example, could we account for the well-established fact that animals engage in food-related activity independent of their immediate hunger state (spiders wrapping prey for future consumption or squirrels storing nuts for the winter)? It becomes all the more evident in the case of reproductive activities such as courting and nest-building. In short, the evolutionary differentiation of meaning units and structures depends upon some degree of functional independence from immediate metabolic needs. While need dimensions at the psychical level may be traced evolutionally and physiologically to underlying metabolic needs, it should be clear that they cannot be *reduced* to them. This underscores our claim that the transition from the prepsychical to the psychical is a profoundly qualitative one.

As the need structures evolve in correspondence with the increasing complexity of the organism and its meaning structures, producing the highly differentiated instinctive action patterns studied by ethologists, it need hardly be stressed that populations and the individual organisms that comprise them are functioning as essentially unitary systems. That is, the emotional assessments, the need dimensions, and the meaning structures evolve in such a way that the parts produced by the differentiation are always integrated into the whole. This is particularly important in the consideration of emotionality because, by Holzkamp's account, emotionality serves the function of mediating between cognition (or proto-cognition) and action. It could not do this in organisms with highly differentiated need dimensions and meaning structures if it did not, at the same time, serve in some sense to unify the necessarily resulting partial assessments, by providing the basis for some kind of overall assessment (which later is experienced as general feeling tone). This is also essential to the individualization of the single organism, which is the ultimate outcome of the early and middle stages of evolution.

COMMUNICATION AND SOCIAL STRUCTURES

Communication is a qualitatively distinct form of interaction among organisms that arises in the psychical stage. The minimal prerequisite is a fairly well-established capacity for discrimination (as discussed above under orientation). It is qualitatively distinct in that it must be more than simply one organism responding to another as part of its environment (as it is all too often treated in most behaviourist accounts). It is a form of *reciprocal* reaction having a 'dialogical structure of information-exchange' (Holzkamp 1983: 113). The 'sender' of information is simultaneously a 'receiver'. Communication is distinguished functionally in that it serves to coordinate the activity of groups. It serves mutual helping, protecting, and supporting, and therefore lends advantages in the maintenance of both individual organism and population systems.

Its evolution involves a functional shift from non-social interactions based on discrimination and the development of other organisms as meaning units into interactions of the social, reciprocal kind. While this makes possible communication *between* species (for example, there is in a real sense communication between prey and predator) it becomes most highly developed *within* species where the increased density of information exchange is most likely to serve the mutual-aid function.

With the establishment of communication, real social groupings become possible. What is meant by 'real' here is that they are based on communication and not merely on attraction to a common environment or to each other as mere aspects of the environment. Social groupings move through a number of forms, from open associations, to which individuals may be added or subtracted according to conditions, to closed associations based on chemical or territorial recognition. The evolutionary unit here is moving away from populations and towards groups. Real recognition, as found in highly differentiated, complexly regulated animal social organizations, requires individual learning, which, in turn, marks the emergence of the individual as significant in itself.

INDIVIDUAL LEARNING AND DEVELOPMENT

The evolution of orientation, meaning, emotionality, needs, communication, and of the social structures that represent the major developments at the prehuman psychical stage culminates in the emergence of individual learning and individual development, which set the stage for the major qualitative shift to the existence of human individuals in society and history. Because of the major significance of this development, it will be useful to present it here in terms of the five steps of the functional-historical method as outlined earlier (which we have not done for the other developments we have described in order to move along more quickly).

Our first question concerns the historically relevant dimensions of the qualitative shift. In this case we note that there is no level of development at which organisms display no capacity for change. There are always ranges of tolerance and variation that provide the variability required by the evolutionary process. The variability occurs first simply as a reflection of the probabilistic, distributional nature of the organismic process and is thus basically non-functional. It can, however, become functional under environmental conditions that favour one range of forms over another. Indeed variability itself may be favoured and passed on as part of the genetic information. This is particularly evident where ranges of variability themselves vary within a species, as when one or the other sex displays greater variability in size depending on environmental conditions. Again at the physiological level, variability in coat colour depending on conditions provides an instance of how physiological variability within individuals can become adaptive.

At the psychical level, it is probably the case that all response patterns are subject to some degree of modifiability depending on external conditions. Habituation of a response would be one example. An organism repeatedly presented with a stimulus, to which it normally displays a fixed, genetically determined response, will eventually quit responding. In some cases, as with the digger wasp, the animal does not cease responding but alters the pattern in adaptable ways (Holzkamp 1983: 123). Such instances are not always referred to as learning, but, however labelled, give clear evidence of the kind of *modifiability*, a combination of fixedness and changeableness, from which learning evolves.

Our second question concerns the evolutionary forces that would encourage the development of individual modifiability at the psychical level. Any understanding of the evolutionary process must assume the working of some sort of efficiency principle, the particular details of which need not detain us here. Clearly, the survival of a species on the basis of a generation-to-generation selection of some and elimination of others (whether organisms or genes does not matter) is much less efficient than survival based on the ability of individual members of a population to adapt to changed or changing conditions. In short, it is easy to see how evolution would favour modifiability of some degree at both physiological and psychical levels of organization. This goes hand in hand with the tendency for organisms to develop more and more complex mechanisms suited to the exploitation of more and more complex environments. Thus the digger wasp evolves a kind of modifiability that allows it to adapt individually to conditions that differ somewhat from those that are normal for the species. Our third concern is to specify the functional shift from modifiable fixed patterns of behaviour to patterns of behaviour that begin to be formed by modification.

Initially, it is simply a matter of individual adaptability to varying external conditions. In the case of the wasp, a subsequent occurrence of the behaviour, if not artificially interfered with, will return to the species-specific fixed pattern. The function of the modification is momentary adaptation. When, however, the inexactitudes of fixed patterns become modified by external pressures to produce a better adapted behaviour altogether, the function of the modification is clearly different. Its adaptive role is expanded and becomes a necessary part of the animal's overall adjustment to its environment. This is the shift from modifiability to learning capacity and marks the origin of a qualitatively new dimension of individual historicity in the life of the species.

To some degree the survivability of the population and of its individual members comes to depend on appropriate modifications. Learning capacity thus evolves as a result of disadvantages that develop in the system of fixed responses, which it then serves to overcome. It evolves not in contradiction to the systems of fixed patterns, but as their necessary extension or adjunct. The possibilities created by the new learning capacity must themselves be fixed or limited by genetic information. Learning, therefore, does not emerge as something that competes with instinct, as appears to be assumed in so many of the learning-versus-instinct debates of the past. As Lorenz (1965) has cogently argued, learning is itself an innate capacity, that is, a new, genetically determined adaptive strategy.

SELF-SUFFICIENT LEARNING AND ITS IMPLICATIONS

For learning to become a *dominant* strategy in the lives of individuals, populations, and species – which is the concern of our fourth analytic step – is, however, a complicated matter that involves at least three distinct substages. The first is one in which fixed patterns remain dominant. Learning develops initially as a capacity that is subsidiary or complementary, and then becomes self-sufficient.[5] The final substage is the one in which learning becomes dominant as an adaptive strategy and a defining characteristic of the species.

The first substage can be traced in the area of orientation and the segregation of the orientational field into meaning units. Habituation, already mentioned, is a very primitive form of this, in which particular units become, at least momentarily, ineffective as stimuli. A more permanent form of acquired selective fixation is found in imprinting, in which the organism is genetically prepared to respond selectively to members of its own species as meaning units, but this becomes (necessarily) still more selectively focused, through an early form of learning, on particular members of the species – usually parents and siblings. Most important, however, are the cases in which various instances of the naturally given meaning units acquire differential valences. Certain locations, for example, become favoured in the orientation of foraging behaviour. This requires both the discrimination of favourable locations from unfavourable ones and generalization of the situational characteristics of the favourable ones. It can be said, therefore, to represent a primitive form of individualized analysis and synthesis of meaning units that represents, in turn, a primitive form of abstractive ability. A more advanced form of this is exemplified in trial-and-error learning.

It should be apparent that to the extent that orientation and meaning structures become affected by learning, so also do emotionality and need-structures. The emotional assessment of meaning units with respect to needs must become individualized if individualized orientation is to be effective. The preferences developed in trial-and-error learning are examples.

It is also obvious that evolutionary development and the complication of communication and social structures is affected by learning. The instance of imprinting has already been mentioned. The most dramatic instances, however, are provided by the complex social organizations of birds and mammals, which at the very least are characterized by some form of dominance relations. These are themselves developed and maintained through learning processes, and, at the same time, clearly imply learned modifications in orientational and emotional processes. The individual member of a social group must reliably respond differentially to other members of the group, which includes assessing, as it were, their valences for the individual.

An important phase in the evolution of learning capacity occurs when it ceases to be merely an advantageous adjunct to genetically fixed patterns and becomes fully self-sufficient. The essence of what happens here is that, while at the earlier substage learning capacity has individualized particular aspects of psychic exist- ence, learning at this middle, 'self-sufficient', substage thoroughly individualizes the psyche itself. One of the most distinctive features of this substage is the appearance of curiosity and exploratory behaviour. The orientational field is no longer constituted simply by meaning units that indicate to the animal 'do this' or 'do that', but now contains a differentiation between such already learned units and *new* units which come to evoke exploratory activity. The animal thus comes to initiate its own learning.

In the emotionality–need dimension this is reflected by an *ambivalence* of new potential meaning units. It is expressed, on the one hand, in the emotional quality of fear; on the other, in the need to control the environment. A new level of emotional assessment arises out of this which might be called 'risk-optimization'. For animals at this stage of development, the world is no longer a range of occasions for executing or not executing some action. It is rather an occasion for constant individual 'decision-making': when and to what extent to approach; when and to what extent to avoid, etc.

An important feature of learning and emotional assessment at this substage is *anticipation*. The new, active nature of learning already implies anticipation that in any new situation there is something to be learned. Likewise, the ambivalence also implies the anticipation of positive or negative outcomes of situations or events that are at the moment neutral. If exploration leads to a positive outcome, the animal comes on future occasions to assess it positively in advance, that is, to anticipate the positive outcome. The reverse is the case for negative outcomes. Critical Psychologists identify this learned, anticipatory, emotional assessment with *motivation*. It is the emotional side of self-sufficient learning. The foraging behaviour of a wasp, for example, may be influenced by learning in both its orientational and emotionality dimensions but this does not yet constitute *motivated* behaviour. Only behaviour guided by the anticipatory emotional assessment that comes with fully self-sufficient learning qualifies as *motivated* behaviour. A fuller justification for this will come with our discussion in a subsequent chapter of motivation at the human level.

As we have already seen, a form of abstractive generalization and discrimination occur at the first substage of subsidiary learning. Self-sufficient learning is accompanied by a significant advance in this regard. Based on a thorough analysis of the experimental ethological and psychological literature carried out by Schurig (1975a, 1975b, 1976), Holzkamp concludes that what emerges here is

> a new level of 'cognitive' information processing that goes beyond 'isolating' and 'generalizing' abstractions and is distinguished by the production of a special psychical relation between classes of abstractable properties [*Merkmalsklassen*] such that an autonomous *internal model* of external relations is formed, which is one of the prerequisites for cognizing states of affairs in their absence and thus for the form of information processing that we call 'thinking'.
>
> (Holzkamp 1983: 149–150)

Such a conclusion is, of course, consistent with what we have already said about the development of anticipation at this substage. Indeed, the exploratory activity linked to anticipation can be seen as aimed precisely at the production and elaboration of these internal cognitive models.

Finally, the shift to dominance of learning over genetically fixed behaviour patterns in the lives of animals is completed with the emergence of social groups. Why is this? While it is clear that self-sufficient individualized learning has distinct advantages for the survival of animal species, it also has distinct disadvantages. At earlier stages in which fixed patterns dominated, an individual animal entered its life with most, if not all, the information it needed for optimal survival already 'built in'. This was obviously advantageous as long as the environmental conditions, however complex, remained relatively constant and the survival of the species was focused mainly on populations. Adaptation to new and changing conditions, however, remained problematic. This was overcome by the gradual development of individual adaptation mechanisms, culminating in self-sufficient learning. The trade-off was that now the individual organism entered its life with insufficient information. Although compensated for by a new capacity to gain needed information on its own, the individual also now faced risks to its life that necessarily accompany mistakes. The development of the social group appears to be an evolutionary compensation for this added risk.

Within this context, further understandable and important developments occur. Perhaps the most important of these is the emergence of the capacity for *individual development*: ontogenesis now assumes major significance in the psychical dimension of animal life. An identifiable young (as opposed to adult) phase of life appears and increases in length with further phylogenetic development. This is necessarily accompanied by increasingly complex social rearing arrangements and patterns of behaviour, such as family groupings and parental behaviour. *Play* develops as a means of learning through exploration within socially protected limits (cf. Braun 1991). Meanings become increasingly determined by the experience of the individual *in the social group*, rather than simply by genomic information or unmediated individual experience; that is, *socialization* becomes an important component of individual psychical ontogenesis. At the highest prehuman levels of this development we see the beginnings of *tradition* acquired through *observational learning*, perhaps the best-documented example of which is that of food washing among Japanese macaques (Schurig 1975b: 131ff, 223ff).

SUMMARY

In this chapter we have moved rapidly through an account of the evolution of the major psychical capacities and dimensions that prepare for the emergence of the human, societal-historical level of existence. This account also provides us with a categorial reconstruction, that is, a set of new definitions of basic psychological concepts. We have seen first what distinguishes the psychical from the non-psychical. We then went on to illustrate how various dimensions of psychical existence become differentiated: orientation and meaning; emotionality and need; communication and sociality. We traced the development of learning out of a more generalized form of modifiability. We noted how learning develops in importance, finally bringing about an important qualitative shift in the way in which animals live in the world and how that, in turn, affects the development of cognitive, social, and ontogenetic capacities.

The central feature of this process is the emergence of the individual as an evolutionary unit. We have seen how this has required developments in the complexity of social organization and can anticipate that it will be a major force in the eventual shift from the merely social to the *societal* mode of existence. The central task of the following chapters will be to show how the understandings that flow from this functional-historical categorial analysis profoundly influence the ways in which we think of the psychical aspects of contemporary human life.

Chapter 6

From phylogenesis to the dominance of sociogenesis

This chapter continues our categorial reconstruction at the societal-historical level of human psychical functioning. We shall first examine the nature of the qualitative transition from prehominid to *Homo sapiens*. This transition is not solely one of psychical functioning, but of the overall process of organic existence in which psychical functioning finds its place. In brief, it is a transition from a dominance of phylogenetic developmental processes to the societal-historical form of development that is both produced by and supersedes phylogenesis. We shall then examine some of the major methodological consequences of this transition. The implications for the fundamental restructuring of psychical categories can then be described.

THE TRANSITION TO *HOMO SAPIENS*

The species *Homo sapiens* is characterized less by the ways in which its biology controls it than by the ways in which it controls its biology. Medicine is an old and familiar example. When non-human animals fall ill, either they recover as a result of natural physiological processes or they die. Some degree of self-initiated intervention may occur, as when a sick animal develops an appetite for a natural substance that assists the healing process. This is referred to as wisdom of the body and is readily accounted for by normal biological, evolutionary development.

The situation is different for human beings who are unique among animals in this regard. When a human being falls ill, other human beings tend to intervene with aid that is guided less by wisdom of the body than by culturally accumulated knowledge handed down from one generation to another, not through transmission of genetic material but through communication and learning. This process ultimately becomes institutionalized in the cultural division of labour as medicine. In our own time, interventions of this sort are becoming quite dramatic: artificially prepared pharmaceuticals based on physiological and biochemical research, X-rays for both diagnosis and treatment, organ transplants, and genetic engineering.

Although animals are known to have 'traditions' that must count as fore-runners of human culture, these do not begin to approach the complexity of human traditions, whether scientific or prescientific. Moreover, animals with traditions are not dependent on those traditions to the extent that humans are on theirs. From a strictly biological point of view, the human animal is effectively over-evolved to a point of being suited only for existence within a culture: humans would not survive without their traditions. On the other hand, if a Japanese macaque fails to learn to wash its food, or a chimpanzee fails to learn how to use sticks to pick grubs out of the crevices of tree bark, their survival and that of their kin and companions is unlikely to be seriously affected.

These are only some of the reasons for believing that the human animal is not merely quantitatively different from other animals (which it certainly is, since much of what humans do is found at least in some less developed form among animals), but qualitatively different. It is this qualitative difference that we shall be concerned with in this section of the chapter. In elucidating this qualitative transition, we shall follow the four steps of the functional-historical method.[1]

In the first step, we can identify a large number of characteristics of pre-hominids that provided the prerequisites for the transition. All these are present among living primates, particularly among the *Pongidae*. We could mention omnivorousness, diurnality, and various developments of the senses both for near and distant objects, but there are three others that appear to be particularly important to our concerns.

The first of these is the capacity for upright posture. Prior to achieving the highest prehominid stage of development, an arboreal environment had served to promote the development of the forelimbs and finally the hands. The upright posture that followed the transition to a savannah environment became a signifi-cant factor, even before it reached the stage of full bipedality, in freeing the hands for the manipulation of objects. Increasing dependence on such manipulation promoted further developments in the fine motor control of the digits of the hand.

The second characteristic followed from the first: the increasing use of objects as means or aids to action. Jane Goodall's observations of free-ranging chim-panzees using sticks to fish grubs from holes is a good example. The experiments by Wolfgang Köhler on captive chimpanzees provide another. It will be recalled that Köhler's chimpanzees were able to rake in a banana by putting two sticks together to make one long enough to reach the desired fruit, and to stack boxes upon which they then climbed to obtain a banana hanging from the ceiling that was otherwise out of reach. A fascinating experiment by Wright (1972) demon-strated that an orangutan could, given optimal conditions and encouragement, learn to make a flaked stone blade to cut strings in order to gain entry to a box containing a desired food.

There are several important observations to be made about these and other examples of tool use by animals. On the one hand, the complexity of the behaviour displayed, as in Wright's orangutan, is often remarkable and from surface appearances alone would be virtually indistinguishable from the broader range of human tool use. What is significant, however, is not merely the use of a tool or other aid but whether the overall activity of the animal consists of distinct phases, each controlled by its relation to a single, common goal. This kind of organization is quite distinct from, and a significant advance over, complex behavioural sequences in which each segment or phase is under the control of a different stimulus, and in which the sequence of the behaviour is more a reflection of the sequence of stimuli – whether given in the environment or produced by the animal's own actions – than of the way in which the animal itself organizes its behaviour. This means for the chimpanzee in Köhler's experiments, for example, that having stacked boxes or put sticks together as aids to action in one situation, these 'skills' now become available for other situations; that is, they are transferable and it is effectively the animal, not the situation, that determines this transferability.

The tools thus produced, such as the sticks used by Goodall's chimpanzees or the flake blades made by Wright's orangutan, are, however, not retained for future use. Whether a chimpanzee uses a stick in a particular situation depends entirely on whether one is available at the time. There is no evidence that these animals go very far from the object of their attention to obtain a tool that is not immediately present, or that they carry such a tool away from the situation of its first use to another situation for which it may be potentially required. In short, while the animal is clearly organizing its own use of the tool, this organization is still to a significant degree situation-bound.

Another observation that can be made here is that the phases of action tend to be organized *within* the individual, only exceptionally among individuals. It is not the case, for example, that one animal stacks the boxes while another retrieves the banana, with the result that the prize is shared. That is, the complex action does not demand or regularly make use of a *social division of labour*. It is important, however, that the social division of labour, with its separation of tool making from tool use and the preservation of tools characteristic of the human being, could not have developed in the absence of these complex developments at the prehominid level.

The social division of labour could also not have developed without the prior development of rather complex, learned social relations at the prehominid level, this being the third major prerequisite for the transition we are concerned with. Again, the higher primate species all display such complex 'interpersonal' relations. The dominance hierarchies appear to be largely biologically based, but they form a kind of framework within which complex learned relations can be formed, such as grooming and even rudimentary coordinations within group activities such as hunting.

Moving to the second step of the functional-historical analysis, what environmental changes could have brought about the contradictions necessary to force our primate ancestors to a yet more complex organization of their activity? Whether forced or voluntary, it is generally agreed among paleoanthropologists (e.g. Wolpoff 1980) that the crucial environmental move was from the forest to open grasslands. With this move came pressure towards the development of full bipedality, greater use and preparation of tools, and significant changes in social organization. The following quotation from Wolpoff identifies some of the important pressures from this new environment.

In a truly open savanna, trees are not available as a means of escaping predation for most of the day, although they might have provided nighttime sleeping refuges. In a primate already using tools, selection for savanna survival could readily lead to dependence on tools for defense. Tools even as simple as clubs make better weapons than canines for at least two reasons. First, they allow fighting at less than extremely close quarters. Second, if clubs are broken, they can be replaced, unlike canines. However, for a club to be useful as a means of defense, it must be immediately available when needed. On an open savanna, this means carrying. Carrying clubs would involve little modification in a hominoid which was already a terrestrial biped, although the behavior might help select for a more efficient pelvic balance mechanism (if it was not already present) because of the weight added to the upper torso. This would result in the loss of any remaining quadrupedal capabilities.

(Wolpoff 1980: 99)

Full bipedality and the use of tools, including their being carried and preserved, also encourages tool *preparation* that begins to approach what might be recognized as *manufacture*, so as, for example, to produce a club of the right proportions and weight. Considering clubs alone, we can already see some important psychological implications. For an animal to carry a stick, it must be able to visualize (or otherwise conceive) its future use. This becomes especially important in the preparation of a club that is heavy enough to be effective against predators but not too heavy to carry. Furthermore, from what we already know about the transferability of skills in existing hominids, it becomes easy to imagine how the relative scarcity of food on the savanna would encourage transfer of the use of clubs for protection to their use in hunting, digging, and rudimentary food preparation. As Holzkamp points out (1983: 166) increased tool use and preparation must result in the 'externalization' of information that animals had already become adept at internalizing (as in emotional evaluation of environmental situations). Information about possible predators, for instance, is externalized in the preparation and retaining of the club that is to be used against them. This also meant pressures on the animal to develop an increased capacity to represent to itself relations extending over both space and time as opposed merely to immediately present stimulus situations. The resulting pressure on the further development and importance of learning need hardly be mentioned.

The move to the savannah also put pressures on social organization. Vestiges of instinctual territoriality would have to be reduced or eliminated as a basis for group cohesion. Ranging over larger areas than in the forest environment, already existing social relationships themselves had to become elaborated to replace territoriality as the primary basis of group cohesion. Carrying of tools led to carrying of food, and this led finally to sharing of food, which must have become an increasingly important basis for social organization. This meant a shift of prominence from biologically necessary familial relations to learned relations based on the preservation of the social group itself. This, in turn, found resonance in the already existing transferability of action phases, so that overall actions could be shared among individuals, as in the collection and subsequent shared consumption of food. Sharing gradually extended to tool preparation and use, such that the preparer or manufacturer needed no longer to be the user. There was probably a positive feedback loop established here in which the need to prepare tools led to the social separation of preparation and use, which, in turn, encouraged more elaborate and extensive preparation.

A general and important outcome of all this is the development of a relationship between the individual animal and its environment that is becoming increasingly mediated by learned social relations and traditions. Individual activity as such became governed more and more by relations to others. The individual had to learn about materials and techniques from others, and the tools produced were shared, as were the products of their use. The activity of individuals was at the same time increasingly governed by activity outcomes that had more to do with the group than with the individuals themselves. This meant significant shifts in the quality of psychical functions such as motivation. Where an animal had been motivated to obtain the anticipated, emotionally most highly evaluated outcome for itself, the outcome now had to be judged in terms of its value for the group because it was only through cooperation with the group that the individual was now able to satisfy its own needs. We shall have more to say about this and other psychical implications later.

The third step in our functional-historical analysis concerns itself with a reversal of means and ends. The reversal significant here is not that of the preparation and use of tools, but of the individual and social relations in which tool preparation and use were embedded. This is reflected in the fact that the needs satisfied by the activity of the group shifted from those solely of individuals to generalized social needs. As we have seen, the pressures that were building in adjustment to life on the savanna favoured closer and more flexible cooperation among individuals for the satisfaction of individual needs. What emerged from this was a transformation of individual needs into social needs. The individual now cooperated not merely for his or her own survival, but for the survival of the group. The group actions that were the individual's *means* for survival become *ends* in themselves, ends now essential to the survival of the individual.

The fourth step was accomplished when this shift in means and ends became dominant. What became dominant was the adaptively flexible, learned manner in which the now essential social arrangements were formed. The result was a major shift from the dominance of biological phylogenesis to historical sociogenesis, that is, to a state that Holzkamp designated as *societal-historical* (1983: 174). This was a shift, as already emphasized, that was not merely one within psychical functioning, but of the entire process in which psychical functioning occurs.

Upon reviewing the apparently necessary steps in the development of the use and making of tools, Holzkamp concludes:

The general principle characterizing this development is the growth in the active appropriation of nature by means of altering, interventional objectification of generalized life-sustaining aims. The objectification thus characterized is the new societal quality of the previously described 'externalization' of orientational activities through the preparation and use of aids to action. . . . The process of appropriation-objectification is the earliest shaping of 'labour' as the creation of use-values in human life; it is the creation of that which makes [human] life possible. Tools are thus the earliest forms of that which makes labour possible.

(Holzkamp 1983: 176)

It is *labour* that is new here. Labour is the collective, objectifying alteration of nature, the control of natural forces for the purpose of providing in advance for the general welfare. This is what distinguishes a *societal* mode of existence from one that is merely *social*. What is objectified here is knowledge about materials and means–end relationships. Thus the appropriation required is primarily that of knowledge, and this is what is handed down through learned traditions.

The knowledge that is appropriated and objectified exists as such in the form of abstractions. Because, as we have already seen, the tool embodies knowledge of its use and of that upon which it is intended to be used, which is its meaning, the tool is the 'carrier' of the historically first, genuine, conscious, reasoned abstraction (which is the same thing here as generalization). At the very heart of the societal as opposed to the social, the societal-historical as opposed to the phylogenetic, is knowledge passed on through learning and tradition, and carried by objects like tools and finally by words.

The crucial precondition for the dominance of the societal is a state in which the internal contradiction between the maintenance of life and external conditions that threaten the life system is no longer resolved through phylogenesis, that is, through alteration in the genomic information, but only through optimizations within the process of forming societal traditions. This is a state that is characterized not by adaptation through the elimination of the least adapted individuals or populations, but through the active adaptation of the societal processes to the demands of the external world. As we have already intimated, this increasingly took the form of altering the external world through learning and the labour process, finally reaching the point of our altering our own biological states.

When was this shift of dominance completed? Schurig (1976) and Holzkamp (1983) see the transitional stages extending from the earliest hominids, probably Australopithicenes, through to the disappearance of *Homo erectus* and *Homo neanderthalensis*, both of whom, they surmise, did not survive precisely because they did not complete the shift to a fully societal mode of existence. *Homo sapiens* developed biologically somewhere around 400,000 years ago (Wolpoff 1980: 247) and probably spent most of the intervening time making the transition.

It is only clear that the transition had taken place when *Homo sapiens* emerged from a hunting-gathering economy (Schurig and Holzkamp call it an 'occupational' economy) to one characterized by agriculture (which Schurig and Holzkamp designate as a 'production' economy). This appears to have occurred only about 10,000 years ago. So, the fully societal *Homo sapiens* is a comparatively recent development. It should be remembered, however, that the societal nature of *Homo sapiens* was under phylogenetic preparation long before the dominance shift occurred. The transitional process, which appears to have taken so long, involved a complex interaction between phylogenetic and societal processes, with the latter finally becoming dominant without any immediate, significant biological change.

METHODOLOGICAL IMPLICATIONS OF THE SHIFT TO SOCIOGENESIS

It should be apparent that, once sociogenesis becomes dominant over phylogenesis, the method we have described as functional-historical is no longer entirely appropriate as a basis for the analysis of psychological categories. Sociogenesis introduces a new 'logic' into the world of human existence which must be reflected methodologically. This is clearly expressed by Wolpoff, who speaks of societal existence as culture:

> [T]he underlying basis for cultural change is very different from the basis for morphological change. Morphological change depends on the forces of evolution acting on existing gene pools. It is tied to the past only in that the genetic variation in the gene pool, which provides the basis of future change, is the result of past history and adaptation. Evolutionary change is linear, and is proportional to the strength of evolutionary forces. The greater the amount of selection, the more rapid the change. But Plio-Pleistocene evolutionary changes have not involved adding *more* genetic material. Instead, the genetic material already present has changed. Cultural change, on the other hand, is tied to the past in a very different way. Cultural change is additive and cumulative. What can change depends on what is already known. The reason Neanderthals did not invent atomic bombs is not that they were 'too dumb,' but that too many ideas had yet to be added to the corpus of human knowledge. What this means is that the *rate* of cultural change must continuously accelerate, whereas the *rate* of morphological change can only respond in a linear way, as it has during the post-Pleistocene. Therefore, there must come a time when the former rate exceeds the latter. At some point, it becomes impossible for any individual within a population to learn the entire body of information that is passed from generation to generation.
>
> (Wolpoff 1980: 354)

It is important in this connection to affirm here that concern for phylogenesis is not being abandoned. As Wolpoff remarks, 'this does not mean that human evolution has ceased; gene pools continue to change' (1980: 355). Indeed, with genetic engineering we are proposing consciously to change them ourselves. Just as Lorenz (1965) successfully resolved the false conflict between 'innate' and 'learned' by pointing out that learning is an evolved and therefore innate capacity, we must keep in mind that the societal mode of existence (or culture) is also an evolved and therefore innate capacity. The point then is not to abrogate the evolutionary, genetically based functional-historical method, but to acknowledge that the dominance of the evolved societal mode of existence creates the need for *additional* methods. To this, Holzkamp remarks that

> the term 'societal nature' as applied to humans is not some kind of pseudo-dialectical trick that by means of paradoxical talk forces together what is in fact irreconcilable; rather, it is the result of demonstrably natural-scientific concept formation.

> (Holzkamp 1983: 187)

As a consequence, our expanded methodology will regard the functional-historical method as the first stage of a two-stage process. Our concern here is to specify the nature of this second stage.

Perhaps the methodologically most important feature of societal existence, as opposed to biological-social existence, is the relation between the individual and the group. When phylogenesis dominates, the information required for the survival of both individuals and the groups (in this case, populations) is genetically coded and carried in the genetic material of each individual member of the population. Variations in this information form the basis of phylogenetic evolution, such that individuals carrying information deleterious to the survival of the population tend to be eliminated, while those whose information serves to advance the survival of the population are preserved. In such a system it is the population that counts most which *must* survive. Individuals are important, but only as elements within the population. Accidental loss of one or more individuals represents no loss of essential information and therefore no threat (except perhaps quantitatively) to the survival of the population.

As the above quotation from Wolpoff indicates, however, matters are different once the human species came to depend on culture, that is, once the societal mode of existence became dominant. In the cultural or societal mode of existence the information required for survival is mostly learned, traditional, or cultural – that is, it is carried in societal relations and not in the genetic material. This information becomes more and more complex, making it impossible for any particular individual to acquire or possess it all. The essential information is shared information, carried from generation to generation in the artifacts and traditions of the society. It now becomes important that individuals are preserved and not just the population. We send trained experts to help our fellow human beings in impoverished Third World countries. Why trained experts and not just anybody? Imagine the consequences of the sudden elimination of doctors and medical scientists from our midst, or the consequences of eliminating all electricians, or plumbers, or farmers. It might be objected that modern technology has removed the skill from many jobs, so that with even minimal skills just about anybody can do them. But somebody had to create the technology that makes that possible. All in all, even cursory reflection on such matters reveals how utterly helpless any one or all of us would be without the support of particular other individuals. In this kind of existence, the societal mode of existence, individuals thus assume a much more important role. The function of society, as opposed to biological populations, cannot be first and foremost to preserve itself; it must be to preserve individuals, and to do this in a planned and conscious fashion.

There is an irony here. Really self-sufficient individuals are those animals who exist only as elements of populations in which they are as such not important. Only as the individual becomes more socialized, societalized, even collectivized, as in the societal mode of existence, does he or she attain to true individuality in the sense of becoming *significant* as an individual. Thus, unlike much popular and scientific thinking stemming from the liberal ideology of individualism (as represented, for example, in Freud's *Civilization and Its Discontents*, 1930/ 1975), the position that we are developing here points to no opposition between society and the individual: it is only within societal relations to other human beings that one becomes an individual (that is, a 'personality'), and society comes increasingly to depend for its survival upon the individualization of individuals (that is, their differentiation as distinct 'personalities').

Strictly speaking, the world in which human beings live is a *societal world*. Hardly ever (if at all) are we confronted by a purely natural world and expected to deal with it on the basis only of information contained in our genetic material. Our relations to the world, both societal and natural, are mediated by our relations to others, whether this be an actual person, an artifact made by other persons, or by language learned from others together with the meaning system carried by language, that is, by knowledge.

Although the functional-historical method can reveal to us the functional basis of psychological categories, it cannot tell us about the *societally mediated character* of these categories at the specifically human societal level of existence. As we shall see, the mediated character of orientation, meaning, emotion, motivation, learning, etc., makes them qualitatively different in significant ways at the human level from their counterparts at the sub- or prehuman level. The second stage of methodology that we are seeking, then, must result from working out the implications of the *fundamental, generalized societal mediatedness* (*gesamtgesellschaftliche Vermitteltheit*) of individual human action.

While this mediatedness can be expected to pervade every aspect of the individual psyche, it is of particular concern to us that it manifests itself in the individual as a distinctly two-sided relationship to societal relations. On the one hand, these relations present themselves to the individual as the pre-existing conditions under which one's personal existence and daily life must be secured; on the other, they present themselves as that which the individual must help to produce and reproduce by taking part in the productive activities related to societal subsistence. The relationship between these two sides of the experienced life-world is itself, of course, societally mediated. Historically, as well as psychologically, it is significant that, as societal existence becomes more advanced (or at least more complex), these aspects of individual lived experience become increasingly separated and potentially discordant. Consider the posting clerk who works for a business firm entering information into a computer from bills of lading and similar documents. Is she thereby securing her own (and possibly her family's) existence or contributing to societal subsistence? Of course, we know, as does she, that she is doing both, but the connection between her actual daily activities and the satisfaction of her needs is a complex one that requires, for example, that she understand that such a connection exists and that she has some reasonable assurance of its effectiveness. Her actions cannot be understood (why, for example, she goes to work at all) from concepts of cognition, emotionality, and motivation that derive from the immediacy of hungry animals responding discriminatively to stimuli for promptly given or even delayed food rewards. According to Holzkamp, the person understood psychologically solely on those terms would be a 'homunculus who could not survive in the real world' (*lebensunfähiger Homunculus*). The cognition, emotionality, or motivation of real people can only be understood in terms of societal mediation, and this requires a theory of how society functions.

Holzkamp moves towards a further concretization of this problem with the observation that

> because individuals maintain their own existence by contributing to the general societal subsistence within a societal structure characterized by division of labour, they never relate to 'society' as a 'whole' directly, but only through the occupation of a *certain position* within the division of labour.
>
> (Holzkamp 1983: 196)

Only by occupying a *position* within the societal structure can the individual contribute to societal subsistence, thereby, under favourable conditions, securing his or her own existence. Societal mediatedness, then, consists of a dynamic relation among at least three factors: the historically determined, overall societal structure (*Gesamtstruktur*); the positions that individuals may assume within the structure and that are historically conditioned components of the structure (*Positionen*); and the immediate life circumstances or situation of the individual (*Lebenslage*). The position of an individual represents a range of *possibilities* with respect both to altering the structure itself and to maintaining and improving the situation. The possibilities of the posting clerk are considerably more limited in both respects by comparison to, say, the chairman of a large corporation. Moreover, some people, occupying no position, have decidedly restricted possibilities, as in the case of the poor and unemployed. We shall see how these factors work themselves out psychologically in due course.

If societal mediatedness substantively affects psychological functioning, and therefore also plays a significant role in defining our psychological categories, and if societal mediatedness is essentially historical in character, we should expect that our psychology will not (indeed, cannot) be independent of the historically specific societal formation.

Societal formations are, according to historical materialist theory, characterized by their mode of production, that is, their forces and relations of production. The broad stages of historically evolving modes of production described by the theory are as follows:

1 Primitive communism, such as probably characterized the earliest human existence after the shift of dominance from phylogenesis to sociogenesis. Earlier we referred to the shift from an occupational economy to a production economy. The division of labour here was probably quite simple, depending in a straightforward manner on what needed to be done and who could do it best. The connection of production to consumption was relatively direct.
2 Slave economy, which represented the first division of labour based on a surplus product. It was the first division of society into classes, one producing the essentials of life and one freed to engage in the elaboration of societal relations through such activities as trade, art, and government.
3 Feudal society, in which the division of mental and manual labour was further developed along class lines.
4 Bourgeois or capitalist society, with an increasingly elaborate division of labour reflecting a rapid expansion of the productive forces.
5 Socialism, characterized by the public and democratic ownership of the means of production. This stage remains a theoretical possibility, although attempts to actualize it in this century have experienced considerable difficulty.

We are now living in what has been called late capitalism, characterized by an integration of state and capital, intense concentrations of wealth and control accompanied by unemployment and poverty, and imperialism with its exploitation and impoverishment of less developed countries, mainly in the so-called Third World.

It is important to see how the variety of *positions*, together with their wide-ranging associated possibilities, has become historically elaborated. In our own time, this elaboration has entailed, more than at any other time in history, the creation of non-positions, that is, an increasing proportion of the population is excluded from productive participation in societal existence. This must be reflected in our understanding of psychological categories. The cognitions, the emotionality, the motivations of any particular individual must be understood in such a way as to reflect his or her position. This is the only way of developing a *concrete* understanding of individuals, as opposed to the *abstract* understandings that see individuals as subject merely to universal laws that are independent of history, societal position, or even species.

BASIC IMPLICATIONS FOR THE HUMAN PSYCHE

As we have already seen, alterations in orientational meanings from fixed to learned and from individual to social are key to understanding the psychologically relevant developments from the simplest animal forms to the highest. As orientational meanings become individually modifiable, learning becomes established as a self-sufficient process. It is also evident that, in connection with this, specifically orientational needs develop that express themselves in exploration and curiosity, and finally in a distinct need to control environmental conditions. All this works itself out in the relationships of individual animals to one another as learned social coordination, in which animals begin to cooperate in the control of environmental events and conditions. For the individual this means an increased loosening of the connection between actually performed activities and individual satisfaction of biological requirements.

Following the first qualitative shift in means and ends, the continued development and elaboration of orientational meanings continue to be of central importance. They play a key role in the development of planful, collaborative production of tools, cooperative survival, and the alteration of conditions in accordance with shared goals of existence maintenance, all, of course, within the dominance of the natural, biological mode of subsistence. We can expect the further development of orientational meanings and its related ramifications to remain of key importance in the second qualitative shift from the dominance of the biological mode of subsistence to the societal mode.

Before outlining the fundamental changes in the human psyche that came with the second qualitative shift, it will be useful first to summarize the significant features of the preceding means–end reversal. The means that became ends, it will be recalled, were what we now call tools. Prior to the reversal, these were, according to Holzkamp, merely aids to action that were recognized by individual hominids as *usable*. With the reversal, these became means of labour, instruments or tools in the modern human sense. They were no longer simply usable but *useful*. Tools in this sense are planfully produced as part of a socially organized effort to satisfy basic needs. As such, a tool is not simply handy for a particular purpose (usable), as is the stick for the chimpanzee who is having difficulty getting the grub from the chink in the bark of a tree; a tool has a *generalized purpose*. It is manufactured with that purpose in mind; it is retained, sought out, and put to use whenever the corresponding need arises. As such it has a quality of artifactuality missing in less developed, natural aids to action, and it created for early hominids a new kind of orientational meaning that would become increasingly important in their lives.

The most primitive meanings, which can be called 'primary', are those associated with the objects that satisfy basic needs. As we have already seen, evolutionary pressures soon produce orientational meanings having largely to do with locating desired objects. With the advent of useful, artifactual tools, there is an elaboration of orientational meanings attached to those tools. Holzkamp calls these 'instrumental meanings' which serve to orient the individual organism to tools, to their uses, and to their manufacture. The artifactuality of instrumental meanings is crucial here. This is precisely what is realized in the activity of making tools. The human activities thus objectified in the tool give it its usefulness or use-value; and these objectified activities, preserved and represented in the tool by orientational, instrumental meanings, are what become realized or actualized in their eventual application. The pivotal role of instrumental meanings becomes clear when we see that they are what must be *anticipated* in the manufacture of the tool, and they are what must be *realized* in its use. Their significance is further underscored by our understanding of their role in the cooperative transmission of socially gained, generalized knowledge. This is essential both to the teaching and learning required for such transmission and to the eventual improvement of any particular type of tool, its differentiation into more specialized tools, and the elaboration of use-values which that implies. Only generalized instrumental meanings make this possible.

The implications for social organization are also profound. With the means–end reversal, the functional division of group activities based on social coordination became a generalized, cooperative division of labour. The recognition of the artifactual, general-purpose nature of the tool implies a simultaneous recognition of others as generalized makers and users. When an individual becomes oriented to the instrumental meanings of a tool, he or she is necessarily being oriented to the actions of others, either as they have been executed in the past (as in using a tool that has already been made) or as they are anticipated in the future (as in making a tool for future use). The other person is now also generalized. Tools are ordinarily manufactured, for instance, for a generalized user, not just for a particular partner in a particular activity (though that is hardly precluded). Instrumental meanings are, in short, meanings for all. The necessary recognition of oneself as a user of a tool or as its maker, together with all that is thereby implied about relations to both particular and generalized others, entails, therefore, a recognition of one's *position* within the general system of social labour. There is a move here from an informed relation to the natural world that merely takes others into account to an organizing, shaping relation between individual and world *within* a generalized social system. This represents a significant step towards a societal mode of existence, and instrumental meanings are essential to it.

There are profound implications as well for the individual's need for control. Before the means–end reversal this was manifested in individuals as a need (with benefits to the population) that merely took others into account. Following the reversal, it was no longer manifested merely as an individual need satisfied through individual curiosity, exploration, and learning of orientational meanings; it became the need of individuals to participate in the social division of labour in order to secure their own existence through the social production of conditions that could assure provision for present and future needs. Basically, the advent of real tools and the social division of labour that they imply meant that survival was no longer merely an individual affair (with whatever implications for the population); it was, rather, an affair of the social group, and it was only through participation in group activities that the individual now survived. This meant a shift from individual activities that were oriented only to making up for one's own wants, reducing one's own distress, or averting threat against one's self, to activities within the social system (i.e. to occupying a position) aimed at creating conditions that could provide security against the possibility of want, distress, or threat. The cooperative division of labour was thus directed not merely at satisfying basic needs under given, natural conditions, but at *creating* the generalized conditions that would assure the satisfaction of needs.

In such circumstances, the *anxiety* of the individual that constitutes the negative evaluation of a deficient or threatening environment becomes converted into an evaluation of the state of affairs within the societal order with respect to the individual. In other words, anxiety came to reflect less the fact that for a particular individual food was not available than the fact that either the social system that normally guaranteed food was breaking down or the individual was becoming isolated from the providing, societal system. On the other side of things, satisfaction could no longer be measured against the bare fulfilment of basic biological needs. The new and more complex socially mediated way in which individual needs were satisfied now meant that the *quality of satisfaction* could only be measured against socially produced *satisfaction possibilities*, which, in turn, served to motivate the further cooperative development of such possibilities.

It was during the period between the two major qualitative shifts that language developed as an aspect of cooperative subsistence. Forms of communication must have been already highly developed prior to the first shift. The ritualization of activities and their acquisition of social signalling function had to be well developed to form a basis for the social coordination that evolved into social cooperation after the means–end reversal. The questions are why and how communication became primarily vocal-acoustic and then symbolic-representational. As we shall see, these two aspects of human language were probably related in their development.

The origin of the vocal-acoustic nature of human communication appears problematic for several reasons. First, there is little intimation of it in other living primates. The well-known experiments on chimpanzee 'language', for example, have succeeded (to the extent that they have) mainly in using gestural signs, not vocally produced sounds. Second, other primates that have moved from the rainforest to savannah-like environments have shown no evidence of pressures to develop acoustic communication. Indeed, there appears to be nothing in either the evidence or the logic of the prehominid move on to the savannah that suggests such pressure. If pressures and apparent biological possibilities are combined, a much better case could be made, on the whole, for the further development of gestural communication.

The pressures for acoustic communication appear to have come not from natural environmental factors, but from the development of tool manufacture. All the implications of this that we have already mentioned point strongly towards the increased need for communication and eventual emergence of vocal language. The shift from the gestural to the acoustic mode can then be seen to reflect the fact that in tool-oriented cooperative subsistence both the hands and the eyes were occupied with the tools themselves. Thus, while pressures for communication at a distance would clearly favour gestural-visual signalling, the proximate nature of cooperative tool-use, combined with its pre-emption of hand and eye, create a distinct pressure for vocal communication.

Once acoustical communication has developed, it is but a short step to the use of sounds for symbolic representation. This is because symbolic representation will already have existed in the instrumental meanings carried by the tools being made and used. As Leontyev put it, it is 'the tool that is the carrier or vector of the first real conscious, rational abstraction, the first real consciousness, rational generalization' (1979: 215). Vygotsky (1978) also made a compelling case for the intimate relation between tool and sign in ontogenesis. Given the generalized, abstract character of instrumental meaning together with the implied functions that we have discussed earlier, it seems quite natural, given the circumstances, that, once formed, these characteristics and functions should be readily transferred to vocally produced sounds. While language as we know it, with all its ramifications for communication and thinking, especially theoretical thinking and knowledge, probably did not develop until after the second qualitative shift, its foundation was laid before that with the development of a wide range of 'practical concepts' carried by acoustic signals.

It is important to keep in mind that everything we have described thus far could, and probably did, develop within a biological, phylogenetic framework. It could only have been biological evolution that shaped organisms that could make tools, live socially, cooperate in labour, and communicate information conceptually by the use of vocalizations. We cannot otherwise imagine how such characteristics would come to dominate the lives of their possessors to the extent that the mode of existence and subsistence thus made possible came to displace the biological mode of existence that had produced the characteristics to begin with. One way of understanding this transition is to imagine that the mode of subsistence had become so complex that it could no longer be sustained simply by information carried in the genome. The tradition-building that had developed as a kind of 'side show' became essential to the survival of the species and its individual members. The information carried by tradition (or culture) was no longer merely supplemental but essential. It reached such a point, and was carried further, because it produced a mode of adaptation infinitely more successful than the phylogenetic one that had produced it. It is to the psychological implications of this second qualitative shift that we now turn.

We can already recognize ourselves in the picture we have sketched out for early hominids prior to the dominance shift. It appears that much of the difference between our immediate ancestors and ourselves is simply an elaboration of what had already been established before the shift. Indeed, biologically speaking, there is little if any difference between *Homo sapiens* immediately before the shift and

now. This must be the case because what we are now, had to have been biologically established well before the shift: presumably it was precisely the
phylogenetic development to a biological state like the one we find ourselves in
that made the shift possible.

Language provides a good example of this. As we have seen, it had to have been
established before the shift in a form that needed effectively only to be elaborated to
be brought to its present form. It is most important that it developed conceptually,
becoming eventually so generalized that today there is no aspect of our world that is
not in some sense meaningful. What is known is named; what is unnamed is not
known. The development of writing appears to have contributed significantly to the
all-pervasiveness of linguistic meaning in our lives. Tools were the first carriers of
humanly produced meaning. With the development of acoustic language in the
context of the manufacture and use of tools, the concepts represented by sounds, and
necessarily translated back into action of the hands in making tools, would sooner or
later find expression in products of manual labour that had no other function than to
carry meaning, such as pictographs and, finally, more abstract visual symbols. The
general result was a world that presented itself to us exclusively in the form of
societally produced meaning structures. The advantages to us have been enormous
from the point of view of the information storage and transmission required by
tradition-formation. We can also see the advantages in problem-solving, the production of new practical knowledge (in which the development of logic and mathematics has played an important role), and, finally, the most abstract and general
theoretical knowledge that allows us to 'know' things about our world that are well
beyond the reaches of the senses themselves.

ACTION POSSIBILITY, ACTION POTENCE, AND SUBJECTIVE
SITUATION

There are three developments that are essential to the further development of our
categorial analysis. These, like present-day symbolic-representational language,
are all characteristics of the new, pervasive *societal* mode of existence and
subsistence; that is, they form aspects of the individual human psyche that can
occur only within an overall societal framework.

The first of these characteristics is what Holzkamp calls *action possibility*.
This sounds quite innocent, but its implications are profound. What we are
referring to here is the fact that the societal human individual does not confront
the world, the sources of need satisfaction, directly. (This is, of course, a development that occurred already before the dominance shift. Its full implications are
felt, however, only after the shift.) At the societal level what the individual
confronts is neither the natural world in itself nor even the natural world mediated
by the actions of others, but the world as a *structure of meanings*. An example
will help to make these distinctions clear. A hungry animal confronted by what it
recognizes (in terms of its primary meaning) as food will generally eat it. The
relationship between the individual animal and the food may be occasionally

complicated by the presence of other animals (hyena in the presence of a lion, or a young lioness in the presence of an older male), but it is still relatively direct. The relationship of the early hominid to food was more complex. The food was obtained in association with others, each performing a different part of the overall task. In the end, moreover, actual consumption resulted from some kind of sharing arrangement. Under socially isolated conditions, we can imagine that such an individual might well revert to a more direct relationship.

Modern humans are different, however. Only under the most extreme and exceptional circumstances is an adult human being likely to revert to the direct relationship that characterizes the prehominid animal. Even alone in the wilderness, we are likely to eat at acceptable times, prepare meals in conventional ways, use knife and fork if available, and even observe ordinary table etiquette. Alternatively, if we are hungry and in the city, we do not simply take whatever food we see. If we did, we know that it would be 'wrong' and most of us would then have to deal with the problem of 'guilt'. The reason for these striking differences between humans and other animals is that we do not confront food as such, but food as part of a societally produced meaning structure. It is not the object that determines our action but the meaning. Meaning, however, does not govern our action in an automatic, reflexive way (as many exceptions to the rule demonstrate); meaning governs what we do as a *possibility for action*.

From a general societal point of view, meaning structures represent all actions required, on average, for the maintenance of societal existence. Meaning structures, from the general societal point of view, then, represent the overall societal *action necessities*. For the individual, however, they always represent *action possibilities*. It is necessary, on average, that someone produce the basic requirements for societal existence, but our shared need for food does not make us all farmers. Some factor will always stand between individuals and the objects of their needs; sometimes this represents a real choice for the individual, sometimes it doesn't. In either case, the relationship is indirect; it can only be characterized as a *possibility relationship*.

An important result of this kind of relation to the world is that it provides, in Holzkamp's words, 'the fundamental material, economic prerequisite for the knowing, epistemic relation of the person to the world' (1983: 236). Basically, the possibility relationship creates a kind of *epistemic distance*[2] between individuals and their world that allows them to assess the relations among events (as opposed to being constantly concerned with the relations of events to themselves), and thus to discover their objective lawfulness. It is in this epistemic distance that we become fully *conscious* of the world and our relation to it. As Holzkamp writes:

> The essential determinant of consciousness in its specifically human form is the emerging epistemic relation of the individual to world and self, materially based on the overall societal mediatedness of individual existential security, in which people are able to relate consciously to meaning structures as action possibilities, thus becoming free of the demands of immediate personal

survival and able to understand the overarching connection between the existential and developmental problems of the individual and the overall societal process by which the means and conditions of providing for human life are created in a generalized way.

(Holzkamp 1983: 237)

The individual thus comes to relate consciously to societal action possibilities, and consequently also to relate as a first person to others in their societal relations. Others can no longer be merely social instruments or communication partners, but necessarily become understood by one as centres of intentionality like oneself. This is the foundation for what we know as *subjectivity*, which is, by this analysis, simultaneously *intersubjectivity*. The reciprocity of societal relations requires that I relate to societal practice from my particular, subjective point of view, and thus to others as acting from their own subjective points of view. Interpersonal relations thus move from a state of mere cooperation to that of a shared subjectivity. Holzkamp observes:

[W]here, under historically defined relations, the other's subjectivity is denied, where the other is treated as a mere instrument and made into an object, where the subjectivity of the other is negated . . ., the 'humanity' of interpersonal relations takes on the character of 'inhumanity' (an animal cannot act 'inhumanly').

(Holzkamp 1983: 238)

The implications for our understanding of the object of psychological investigation are important. An animal may be treated experimentally, scientifically as an object of our knowing activity. We do not stand in an intersubjective relation to animals. With other human beings, however, we do: the psychologist is also a subject. Psychology as a subject-science is, therefore, a peculiar science and this peculiarity must be reflected in its categories and methodology if it is adequately to fulfil its scientific mission. These are points that will be developed further in the following chapters.

The second characteristic of the societal mode of existence that will be important, perhaps the most important, to psychology is *personal action potence*.[3] We have already discussed in some detail the complex, societally mediated relationship that the individual has to the world. We have also discussed the development of the need for control, both on the part of society itself and on the part of the individual. Out of this emerges a picture of the individual as highly dependent on society for the degree of control that he or she will actually have over personal learning and development, and over the satisfaction of needs generally. Personal action potence is basically the control that an individual has of his or her own conditions of life through participation in the generalized control of the societal process (cf. Holzkamp 1983: 241).[4]

The significance of personal action potence in societal existence is made clear by the exception Holzkamp takes to Marx's claim that 'labour is the first vital need'. To this Holzkamp replies:

It is not 'labour' as such that is the first vital need, but 'labour' only to the extent that it gives the individual a meaningful part in the control of the societal process, that is, to the extent that it makes the individual 'action potent'. Consequently, it is not 'labour', but 'action potence' that is the first vital need.

(Holzkamp 1983: 243)

Returning to the problem of anxiety, we can see that it is a result of action *im*potence caused either by a breakdown in society or by the isolation of the individual from the societal process. Personal action potence (or impotence) will obviously reflect the particular societal formation in which the individual lives, the ways in which power is exercised in that society, etc. These are matters that will receive further attention in the next chapter, in which we shall also learn how action potence may assume different forms.

The third and last psychological characteristic of societal existence that we shall mention here is *subjective situation*.[5] We have already seen that, early in phylogenesis, emotion developed as a kind of subjective standard for assessing the immediate environment with respect to the satisfaction of needs. Subjective state is the societally evolved form of this. The individual whose 'first vital need' is personal action potence, and who is confronted by a complexly mediated world in the form of meaning structures offering possibilities for action, needs some way of assessing his or her own position in the societal process. As in emotion, subjective state is a reflection or assessment of the objective situation of the individual. This is achieved, however, through a reflection or assessment of one's relation to self. It is the experience of self that is ultimately a gauge of the person's quality of life. It should be clear that this will be relative both to the societal formation in which the individual lives and its historical stage of development. This and other points will be elaborated in the following chapter.

Chapter 7

Individual subjectivity and its development

The world for which individual human beings are biologically prepared by evolution, and into which they must develop, is a societal one. It is a world of meaning structures, not a 'natural' world in the usual sense of the word. This dependence on meaning, as we have seen in the preceding chapters, creates for us an epistemic distance[1] from the world. This means that our actions with respect to it are consequently mediated by meaningful reflection. We do not act with respect to the objects of our world – whether they are actual things, complex situations, values, ideas, or ourselves – reflexively or out of some other form of natural necessity. While for societies there are necessities for action, these have an 'on average' character, and thus present themselves to us not as necessities but as possibilities for action.

When our relation as individuals to our world is one of possibility instead of necessity, our actions are no longer simply determined by objects (or by others or even ourselves) as stimuli. Rather, our actions are *grounded* in meanings regarding objects as goals of action. We thus speak of the *grounds* of our actions. As we shall see, this does not imply that all action is necessarily rational or that the grounds on which we act are our own or even in our best interest, nor does it imply that actions cannot be carried out thoughtlessly or automatically.

The *possibility relationship* that we are describing provides the context for the development of individual human subjectivity. The present chapter will be concerned with a further elaboration of the nature of this relationship, along with the two essential characteristics to which it gives rise: *action potence* and *subjective situation*. Having done that, we shall turn to a consideration of some important aspects of the development of individual subjectivity.

THE POSSIBILITY RELATIONSHIP

As we have already seen, unlike animals, individual humans do not seek to make their existences secure by responding in an unmediated fashion to the demands of their environments, even when these are understood as meanings. Instead, the demands of life present people with alternatives, the most basic form of which is to act or not to act. In this respect individual humans are free. To most of us, of course, freedom means much more than this alone, but such an elementary freedom is fundamental to the more complex kinds that become elaborated in the course of human history. There is, however, another side to the possibility relationship considered as freedom, and this is, as we all know, that the latitude of freedom in any society can be restricted, suppressed, and deformed. Where this occurs, however, the possibility relationship is not extinguished. The possibility relationship is an *essential* characteristic of the human species and can be objectively annihilated only with the species itself. Objective possibilities for humans, therefore, always exist in principle. We shall have more to say about this after we have examined *action potence* and *subjective situation* more closely.

In the possibility relationship lies the fundamental prerequisite for the individual human's reflective, knowing relation to the world. It is through the 'existential unburdening', implied by the fact that individuals are no longer required to respond to the meaning of every event touching their lives, that epistemic distance arises (Holzkamp 1983: 236). It is this distance that makes possible the comprehension of the lawfulness of the objective order. In this connection, Holzkamp takes issue with the usual Marxist understanding of what distinguishes human consciousness:

> The connection of the cognized interrelations to the material maintenance of life does not get lost here [in this epistemic distance]; it is rather just as mediated as the connection between the assurance of individual and societal life in general. It is therefore insufficient to define consciousness merely as the individual capacity for planning through anticipation of generalized outcomes of labour (as in Marx's well-known example of the architect and the bee [in which the architect is distinguished by a mental construction that precedes actual construction]). It is just as insufficient to equate consciousness with the mediation of mental contents through the appropriation of societal objects or their linguistic-symbolic representations. The essential, defining characteristic of consciousness . . . is rather the cognized world–self relationship that emerges materially out of the comprehensive societal mediatedness of the individual assurance of life – in which people can relate consciously to meanings as possibilities for action – that releases them from the immediate demands of life maintenance, making them capable of comprehending the overall connection between the requisites for individual life and development and the process by which the means and conditions for the preservation of human life are created in the societal process.
>
> (Holzkamp 1983: 236–237)

Only on the basis of this fundamental comprehension, this new quality of *consciously-relating-to* societally created possibilities for action does it become feasible for the individual to plan and anticipate particular outcomes of his or her own labour, that is, to reveal the characteristics that we associate with consciousness.

This consciously-relating-to possibility for action has one other important implication that should not go unnoted here. This concerns how we relate to other humans and to ourselves. The relating involved here is a personal relating; it is always in the first person. This very fact creates the necessity for a sharper distinction between the self as knower and the object known, thus simultaneously creating an increasingly acute sense of oneself as knower, as a genuine *centre of intentionality* (Holzkamp 1983: 238). But this first-person subjectivity emerges only in a context of cooperative and communicative interrelations with other people, that is, in a set of societal relations characterized by their reciprocity.

At the level of the conscious relating-to the reciprocity of social relations assumes the human quality of *reflexivity* by which, from the standpoint of *my* world- and self-views, I simultaneously take into account *the other's* world- and self-views, such that a level beyond that of simple social manoeuvring is achieved, namely that of the *reflective entwining of perspectives* that is characteristic of the human species.

(Holzkamp 1983: 238)

Individual subjectivity, in short, emerges simultaneously as human *intersubjectivity*. From this point of view, the so-called problem of other minds never arises.

There are some obvious implications for psychological method of considering subjectivity as entailing intersubjectivity. These stem from the recognition that the researchers, like the persons they traditionally call 'subjects', are also subjects. We shall examine some of these implications in the next chapter.

PERSONAL ACTION POTENCE

Possibilities for action are simultaneously possibilities for the satisfaction of needs. It is not merely that individual actions are mediated; the relationship between individual needs and societal meaning structures is mediated at the same time.

On the whole, the definitive moment in the 'humanization' of the meaning–need relationship . . . is an alteration in the mode of environment control. At the preceding phylogenetic level of individual capacity for learning and development there developed a mode of control of the individual environment through learned orientational meanings, linked to the emergence of a basis for satisfying needs that regulates tendencies of approach and avoidance with respect to novelties and resistances in the world of objects and other animals in a biologically meaningful way. In the course of developing the societal nature of humans the direct, individual control of the environment was gradually converted by societal labour to a generalized mastery of tools within a cooperative production of the means and conditions required for life. Thus learned orientational meanings became instrumental meanings and the need for control correspondingly became more specifically the elementary individual necessity for participation in the cooperative mastery over the requirements for life, and thus also over the primary satisfaction of needs and alleviation of anxiety through the foresightful securing of societally created sources of need satisfaction.

(Holzkamp 1983: 240)

Most individual non-human animals bear the responsibility of dealing on their own with the environment in such a way that their basic needs are satisfied. More highly evolved animals develop modes of cooperative behaviour that enhance the individual's chances of success in this endeavour. But even under highly co-operative modes of social existence, individual animals live in an essentially unmediated relationship to their natural environments. The societally mediated relationship that replaces this immediacy for humans creates an entirely different situation with respect to the satisfaction of needs. The pertinent control is no longer direct at all, but achieved only through association with others. We satisfy our needs, not by dealing directly with the environment, but by taking part in a societal process of ensuring in advance that human needs in general will be met. Primitive agriculture provides a clear example. People work together to produce more food than they can immediately consume at a particular time, with a major share of the product being stored for future use, on the understanding that all those who participated in production will have access to the food as needed.

A particular individual may shuffle papers in a corporate office all day. These papers do not satisfy needs for food, clothing, shelter, or transportation, not to mention aesthetic and other cultural needs. If that person needs food, it is found in the local market; clothing too is found in a local store; a flat can be arranged through the appropriate broker; cars, buses, trains, and planes are available for getting around; theatres, art galleries, radio, television, and the cinema provide for other needs. An important implicit understanding, in this instance, is that the paper-shuffling that the person does contributes in some real way to the main-tenance of the system of need satisfaction. Participation in the general system of assuring the satisfaction of needs earns for the person, through the medium of wages, the 'right' of access to the system at a level that, under ideal conditions, reflects the extent of his or her contribution.

The most important expression, then, of the individual's possibility relation-ship to the environment is the possibility of participation in the general system of need satisfaction. This is *personal action potence*, which Holzkamp variously defines as 'participation in the control of the general process of societal pro-duction and reproduction, including the particular requirements relevant to one's own life' (1983: 240) or 'the exercise of control by the individual over his or her own requirements of life through participation in the control of the societal process' (1983: 241). This participation can be complicated and distorted in some obvious ways that stem from the exercise of economic and political power by others. We shall deal with some of these problems in a later section of this chapter.

SUBJECTIVE SITUATION

It is one thing to be able to participate in a societal system in order to satisfy one's own needs; it may be quite another to satisfy those needs and to assess the satisfaction accurately. It is therefore necessary to consider the phenomenal, experiential side of the subjectivity that we have just introduced as personal action potence. This experiential side is referred to as the individual's *subjective situation*.

> In the possibility relation to general societal meanings the needs are not merely emotional states or variables that lead immediately to need satisfying actions through the actualization of meanings. Rather, more than that, they constitute an 'intermediary' between particular actions, in which the subject experiences his or her own need state, emotional readiness for action, perplexity, or the like in the context of particular available possibilities for or restrictions on action. The action here, being the realization of the conceivable possibilities for action within a given pattern of meanings, only occurs as the result of consciously 'relating-to' one's own situation as the subjective reality of actual emotional assessment of the meanings. The subjective situation is therefore the specifically human form of the mediation between cognition and action as described earlier. It is the 'yardstick' of the degree and kind of need on the basis of which the individual decides to what extent the generally available societal action possibilities must be subjectively realized for the particular individual, or to what extent objectively existing restrictions on action affect the individual possibilities for life and satisfaction.
>
> (Holzkamp 1983: 244–245)

The subjective situation is thus a personal assessment of one's own action possibilities, of where one stands in a particular objective situation. It is thus an assessment of the actual, objective environment, but it is simultaneously an assessment of one's self in that environment. It is not uncommon to find different people assessing exactly the same objective situation differently, usually on the basis of past experience in similar situations. It is perhaps best viewed as an assessment of one's *personal relationship* to the environment with respect to the action possibilities that are *effectively* available to the particular subject.

Emotion plays an obviously important role here. But it is not emotion alone, even in its assessment function, that defines the subjective situation. It is the *conscious* relation of the individual to his or her own emotions that is important. It is this conscious 'relating-to' one's own emotions that supplants the immediacy of the relationship between needs and action found in the prehuman condition and lends a significant subjective aspect to reality (cf. Holzkamp 1983: 318, 324).

DETERMINATION VERSUS GROUNDEDNESS OF ACTION

The fact that we live in a possibility relationship to our world requires a special understanding of how we account for our actions. Why did so-and-so act in such-and-such a way in that particular situation? The kind of answer we have generally been prepared to expect from the psychology of this century is one in terms of stimulus, response, and reinforcement. The environment is conceived as a collection of stimuli that either directly evoke or set the occasion for a response that has previously been reinforced or rewarded in the presence of particular stimuli. This kind of account is based on the assumption that action or behaviour is *determined* by the environmental stimuli. In the case of evocation (or, in Skinnerian terms, the response considered as 'respondent') there is a direct causal link between the stimulus and response. Most 'instrumental' responses, however, require further conditions for their occurrence (where Skinner would speak of 'operants'). The immediate stimulus (discriminative stimulus) is said to 'set the occasion for' the response, which may or may not occur depending on such factors as the state of the organism. Variable internal conditions may, for instance, form part of the necessary 'stimulus complex': for example, the pigeon does not eat when presented with food unless it is hungry. The operant account, however, is still determinist and causal in the mechanistic sense of the terms. The only difference between the respondent and operant conceptions lies in the presumed complexity and variability of the causal event.

Given our analysis of human action in a possibility relation, this kind of account requires significant modification if we take the term 'possibility' seriously. If societal mediation and subjectivity as we have elaborated them create and require a new kind of relationship to the environment, we will need a new account of what determines action, that is, a new expectation regarding the answer to our question of why people do what they do. For one thing, it should be obvious that the standard account of action as caused is precisely an account that, at best, reflects an *unmediated* relation to the world such as one might expect of prehuman (particularly 'lower') animals.

If we live in a possibility relation to the world, we must have alternatives with respect to the action taken, or even whether we act or not. There must exist for any instance the possibility of having acted otherwise. It is this condition that lends a peculiarly human sense to words like choice and freedom. If these senses represent anything real – and it follows from the Critical Psychological categorial analysis (not to mention our own personal experiences) that they do – truly human actions are not determined through ordinary mechanical causation but are rather accounted for by the actor's *grounds for action*.[2] Grounds for action derive from our assessments, both emotional and cognitive, of our environments and of the possibilities for action that they offer and that we recognize. Grounds for action provide the immediate explanation for action, and they are part of our subjective states. This rootedness of grounds in the subjective situation is related to the epistemic distance we spoke of earlier. It is in this 'space' between us and objects that grounds for action develop as distinct from mere stimuli. It should also be apparent that the subjective groundedness of action is essential to such aspects of societal existence as invention, innovation, and personal creativity.

We have said that personal subjectivity is at the same time intersubjectivity. This means that grounds for action must be intelligible not only to ourselves but to others. As we have argued (and substantiated) in our categorial reconstruction of the societal nature of the human psyche, subjectivity arises only within a human societal context. The meanings that make up my grounds for action are thus originally those found in the objective meaning structures of my societal world. They become mine in the course of development and continued action in this world through a process of appropriation. I may have considerable latitude with respect to what I personally do with them, but this does not alter their fundamentally societal nature. Grounds for action are, therefore, essentially *generalizable* grounds for action, and, as such, are always subjective-intersubjective grounds for action.

Insofar as my actions are in fact grounded for me in my needs and interests, they must in principle be recognizable to others, and thus be intersubjectively intelligible. Because I am myself an instance of the generalized other and an other for others, my efforts at making sense of myself through the adequate grounding of my actions is identical to the efforts of others to achieve sensible grounds for their action. If I am unable to ground my actions for others (through reference to subjective needs and interests), then I cannot ground them for myself (out of which situation arises the necessity for after-the-fact justification of actions through the manufacturing of a context for grounding, sometimes at the cost of subjectivity's loss of reality).[3]

(Holzkamp 1983: 350)

Holzkamp concludes that the generalized nature of groundedness and of its intelligibility is a necessary and essential prerequisite for the individual's inclusion in any aspect of societal life, but particularly in that of societal production.

What all this means is that, as human beings, we live in an essentially objective and shared nexus of meanings in which we participate through appropriation and shared action. There are, of course, instances when the actions of others and even of ourselves appear to be unintelligible, but intelligibility must always exist in principle. Holzkamp describes an everyday example of this:

[I]f I see someone approaching with a hammer in hand, a nail between his teeth, and a picture under his arm, it is normally clear to me from our common experience in life that he wants to hang the picture. His inwardness [subjectivity] is thus for the most part no problem for me, since what he at the moment feels, thinks, and wants, externalizes itself in its practically relevant aspects for me out of his meaningful action. If he does something unexpected (contrary to hypothesis) [and] puts the hammer away, spits out the nail, leans the picture against the wall, and walks quickly away, then he is still not really puzzling or incomprehensible. I assume that I am unaware of the particular *premises* of his new action, which nevertheless remains in principle understandable for me. I therefore ask him, in case he has not already offered some pertinent explanation, 'What are you doing?' He will probably reply, 'The milk's boiling over', or something of that sort, and with that, things are again clear to me. But even if he does not answer, although he must have heard me, there normally remains in everyday practice an easily testable hypothesis stemming from our common context of life and meaning. Even the extreme case of an inwardness that is shut off from me does not signify incomprehensibility or meaninglessness, but may even possibly have an especially serious and momentous meaning within the context of our shared life.

(Holzkamp 1991a: 72)

Holzkamp speaks here of the picture hanger's *premises* for action. We have seen that the most immediate determinant of an action is its subjective ground. We have also seen that subjective grounds for action are necessarily intelligible in principle, both for ourselves and for others. To complete the picture (or sketch, since there remains a good deal more to be said than we can get into the presently allotted space; see Maiers 1993), we need to fill in the connection between grounds for action and the real world in which we live. This real world, which includes the everyday conditions of our lives (to which belong the presumed causes and stimuli of behavioural psychology), yields the premises of our grounds for action. We do not respond directly to them as such, but only as they are reflected subjectively in our grounds for action. They do, however, form the real context of our actions and ultimately determine both the possibilities for and restrictions on our action. It is, after all, the real physical and social world that we are ultimately having to deal with, and that stands at the other end of the possibility relation that creates subjectivity in its inward and outward forms, and with the various features we have described.

SUBJECTIVITY IN SOCIETY

Subjectivity in the truly human sense arises only in society, but this is hardly all that needs be said about its relationship to societal existence. We have yet to specify the influences of the structural features of society on the forms taken by individual subjectivity.

At the heart of the individual–society relationship is the problem of satisfying needs. We satisfy needs by producing those things which do the job. But we don't all do the same thing. Societal production is a complex business, each person performing only some small part of the overall task. Obviously, the end result must somehow work out for each and every participant to one degree or another; that is, the amount and diversity of the total product must, on average, approximate the extent and diversity of individual needs in the population. This requires an organization of arrangements, understandings, laws, mores, and the like, which yields *positions* for its individual members. What we are calling 'position' roughly approximates what is usually called 'role', 'job', 'function', or 'niche'. It represents a contribution of the individual necessary for the functioning of society as a whole.

To a large extent it is the position that determines the immediate *life situation* of the individual. This is the 'place' in which each of us always finds him- or herself. It is the house I live in, the people with whom I live, work, and play, the stores in which I shop, etc. It is, in short, the immediate world in which I find my satisfactions, frustrations, amusements, etc. It is a small spatial-temporal slice of the overall societal structure and process of which I am a part.

Bourgeois society is characterized at one level by its division of labour and, at a broader level, by its class structure which is tied to the relations of production. The life-world of the mine-owner is literally different from that of the miner. The two occupy different points within capitalist relations of production. They perform different functions in the division of labour. In short, they occupy different *positions* in society and thus experience different *life situations*. This is bound to have significant effects on subjectivity, or, more specifically, on the action potences and subjective situations of the two individuals.

On the one hand, the differences between the mine-owner and the miner can be characterized in purely quantitative terms. The owner is sure to have a much wider scope of action possibilities, greater numbers of opportunities for need satisfaction (indeed, even more 'needs'), greater assurance of continued participation in the societal production process (for example, in a tight coal market, it's the miners who are laid off, not the owner), and greater power altogether (owners decide the fates of miners more easily within our societal norms than vice versa). These real, objective differences that stem from their different positions are reflected and experienced subjectively in their respective life-situations as distinctly larger or smaller *subjective possibility spaces*.

It is, however, the qualitative side of these differences that brings us to one of the most important and useful distinctions that Critical Psychology makes regarding subjectivity: the difference between *generalized* and *restrictive action potence*. The difference begins in what Holzkamp calls the 'double possibility' (1983: 367). In order to understand this, we need to move back from the individual for a moment to the movement of society as a whole through time. We call this 'history', which is the continuing elaboration of the possibilities inherent in the societal mode of existence once it emerges in evolution. On average, the overall possibilities for action and the conditions that support them have expanded enormously over time. We see this in the exponential development of technology, to mention but one important aspect of societal existence. Although this expansion is a societal process, it comes about only because of the participation of individuals collectively innovating, inventing, discovering, trying, testing, and producing. While society appears to have no choice in the matter since further expansion of possibilities is necessary for its continued existence, this is not the case for individuals. Individuals as such always have the choice, which they may or may not make for themselves, extending the limits of their existing possibilities for action or living within existing possibilities. How, then, does this affect personal action potence, and thus also the subjective situation? We have defined personal action potence as the exercise of control by the individual over the conditions relevant to the satisfaction of his or her needs through participation in societal production. As we have seen, it belongs to the very nature of the human species that each and every individual member of society has action potence. Every individual person has, in principle (that is, theoretically, though abstractly), the fundamental capacity to extend his or her own and others' possibilities through cooperative action. It is also in his or her interests to do so, since it is necessary for the continuance of societal existence and it contributes to the continued improvement and safeguarding of his or her own quality of life.

The potential for restrictions on individual extension lies in the structure of society. Each individual can deal with only part of the action, that is, each must occupy a position in society. On the positive side, it is precisely through their positions that individuals both contribute to and benefit from the societal extension of possibilities. One's position can, however, be limiting simply because the individual in it does not command all the skills, knowledge, or physical or mental capacity to do all that is necessary to extend his or her own possibilities. Obviously, then, any degree of isolation of an individual in his or her position will result in a diminution in the objective capacity to extend possibilities. What this emphasizes is the necessity for organized, conscious, and unhampered co-operation among individual members of society for effective extension of individual possibilities. In any case, what particular action is grounded for any individual will always depend on his or her position, its related life situation and the premises it allows for the grounding of action. Another way of saying this is that individuals can and will do only what for them is *subjectively functional*.

SUBJECTIVE FUNCTIONALITY

Subjective functionality of grounds for action is especially conspicuous when individuals appear to limit themselves with respect to the extension of their possibilities. For one thing, it must be recognized that, since all action takes place within possibility relations, the possibility not to act or to act in a way that merely uses rather than extends available possibilities must exist in principle. This, coupled with the fact that individual actions are not caused by external conditions directly but always grounded subjectively, allows us to see that it is at least possible, owing to a multitude of both objective structural and subjective personal grounds, that individuals may choose not even to take up their objectively available possibilities, let alone attempt to extend them. The question here, as above, is what grounds for action are subjectively functional for the individual.

What becomes subjectively functional for any particular individual, and why, are important questions for us. We can deal here with only the most obvious determinants. One of these is the inherent risk associated with, and effort required by, any attempt to go beyond what already works. Holzkamp speaks of a pervasive contradiction between anticipated improvement and risk in every action directed at extending the exercise of control over the conditions of one's own life.

Extending the possibilities for control over conditions and thus also of action potence always includes the giving up of an existing state of relative action potence (however inadequate it is experienced to be) together with its proven means of coping with life and the demands of one's position; an attempted improvement in the quality of life through a higher level of relative action potence is always linked (more or less) to an existential insecurity over whether or not the higher level can actually be achieved, and, if not, whether the present lower state of action potence will itself be lost in the process.

(Holzkamp 1983: 371)

Of course, considering the societal situatedness of individuals, such risks can be minimized or even eliminated in an ideally functioning society through co operative support. This ideal state, however, does not exist in a society such as our own in which positions are associated with classes, and classes with power and dominance. Clearly, the risks are very different for the mine-owner and the miner, and the difference is maintained and enhanced by the dominance of the mine-owner. It is not difficult to imagine that when the owner's dominance over the miner's life circumstances is, as it must be, included in the latter's premises for action, the corresponding subjective grounds for action may understandably be reduced and limited to the mere utilization of available possibilities rather than to their extension. Active extensions of his or her own possibilities may be effectively *non-functional* from the miner's subjective point of view.

What Holzkamp calls the 'central moment' of this entire process is this:

The alternative of extending control over conditions can only be subjectively grounded and functional when, along with the possibility for extension, the individual experiences at the same time the possibility of averting the antici- pated endangering of his or her existence, that is, by achieving a counter-force through cooperative combination with others that is of such a size that the danger to the existence of each individual is neutralized.

(Holzkamp 1983: 373)

It should be clear from this, and what has already been said, why dominance is most often exercised in society not by brute force but through ideological means that have the result of isolating the dominated, not only from the sources of power but also from one another (consider the widespread and intense hostility towards trade unions, not only among capitalists but often among working people them- selves). Ideological domination can have exactly the same effects as brute force in limiting what is subjectively functional for the individual with respect to grounds for action. The cooperative relations necessary for genuine extension of action possibilities and thus for the improvement in the quality of life are replaced with competitive relations. Relations with others are all reduced to relations of power and dominance. Where the relative power is more or less equal, too equal to allow actual dominance, interaction becomes based on *com- promise* (if you give in a bit for me, I'll give in a bit for you) and *compensation* (if you give me something of yours that I want, I'll give you something you want in return). Intersubjective relations become relations in which individuals are reciprocally instrumentalized for the sake of strictly personal interests. Indeed, all interests are reduced to personal interests with a consequent loss of any sense of the collective interest.

GENERALIZED AND RESTRICTIVE ACTION POTENCE

But the real chances for extending both societal and personal action possibilities are never entirely sacrificed. They cannot be suppressed completely if society is to survive. Even the most self-centred capitalist has an interest in overall growth of the economy. Moreover, the dominant cannot retain their dominance for long by brute force or empty ideology alone. A real possibility must exist for individuals to improve their lot. Here we must return to our distinction between *generalized* and *restrictive action potence*. *Generalized action potence* is generalized because it exists for one as for all. It would be the only kind in an ideal society, but as an analytic category it applies as well to less-than-ideal bourgeois society. It does not characterize individuals as such – that is, it is not like a personality trait – and does not even characterize positions or classes. It is better thought of as a characteristic of instances within the generalized network that includes subjective grounds and possibilities for action. The same must be said of its opposite, *restrictive action potence*, which is restrictive because it confines its benefits to particular individuals, though not without costs to them, and always at a cost to others and to society as a whole.

Whereas in generalized action potence the individual gains his or her power through cooperative participation in societal production, in restrictive action potence the power is gained through participation in the power of the dominant forces in society. An extreme example would be the young Central American peasant who finds that he can improve the quality of his own existence by joining the army, thus moving rapidly from the status of the oppressed to that of oppressor. More ordinary examples are the numerous instances familiar to us as characterized by the phrase, 'if you can't lick 'em, join 'em'. However extreme or ordinary the instance, it contains an important contradiction. On the one hand, restrictive action potence is subjectively functional for individuals in a society like ours. On the other hand, to one degree or another it constitutes a denial of the true societal interest, and to that degree, owing to the fact that in the final analysis our individual interests are identical to the collective societal interest, it puts us in a position of hostility towards ourselves. This cannot help but lead to 'disturbances' of a clinical nature.

For our present purposes, the single most important psychological feature of this strategy is the subjective identification of one's own interests with those of the dominant, and the interests of the dominant with those of society. Ideologically, this identification is made so pervasively as to appear to represent natural law itself. Taking advantage of other people, instrumentalizing all social relationships, 'looking out for number one', are taken to be expressions of unalterable 'human nature'. The implications for cognition, emotion, motivation, and the unconscious are of special interest.

THE UNCONSCIOUS

The ways in which we think, the cognitive competencies required for the appropriation of societal meanings, how we feel about things, why we choose to act in one way rather than another, can only be comprehended in terms of that which for the given individual is subjectively functional. As we have seen, what is subjectively functional is always ultimately rooted in a person's position and life situation, and thus in the societal structure in which he or she is a participant. This means that our present considerations must begin with a recognition of our own existence in bourgeois society, a society that has the capacity to employ everyone usefully, yet does not; that can prevent hunger, yet does not; that can find ways of providing for human needs without destroying the environment, yet does not; and so on. We are, each of us, compelled by the mere fact of our existence in this society at this historical moment to participate in a society in which the interests of a dominant few are put forward as the interests of all, but when they, in fact, are not. Indeed, the dominant interests quite plainly run contrary to the general societal interest: the concentration of wealth and power in the hands of a few is not necessitated by societal or individual human interest in general; it has rather proved itself over and over to be highly destructive both to the lives of innocent individuals and to the physical and societal world in which we live.

Participation in societal production and reproduction, such as it is, requires each of us to accept their associated conditions to some extent or another. We cannot refuse to participate because we do not approve: it is, as they say, the only show in town, and our lives quite literally depend on it. To the extent, then, that real individual interests are identical with general societal interests and our everyday existences are dependent on our accommodating an historically distorted version of these interests, we are caught in an objective contradiction in which the furtherance of some of our interests (such as bare survival) can only be accomplished at the expense of others (such as full development and productive utilization of our talents). In short, we are caught in historical circumstances in which we must, to one degree or another, deny and/or violate our own (and thus also general societal) interests; we are forced into a state of self-hostility.

Critical Psychology sees this historically produced distortion as the basis for the unconscious. The unconscious is accordingly not an 'anthropological given' (Holzkamp 1983: 381) nor is it irrational. It is rather the exploitation by a particular societal configuration of the individual human capacity to repress the fact that what one is forced to do runs counter to one's interests. From this point of view the unconscious would appear to be quite 'rational' in that it responds realistically to the demands of the life situation and to the subjective functionality of grounds for action. From our analysis of subjectivity in society, it can be characterized as a built-in assurance of a relatively risk-free individual existence. Of course, repression succeeds in varying degrees, which will become important in our further considerations.

COGNITION

Cognition or thinking begins in our life situation, in the world that we grow up in and into, and in which we must negotiate our way from day to day. We must not lose sight of the fact that this is a world characterized by fundamental contradictions of interests that reflect imbalances in dominance and power. It is also the case that we must, to some degree or another, accept our world as it is, both physically and ideologically, in order to meet our basic needs. Corresponding to our real and ever-present alternatives either to act only in accord with our life situation (utilization of its possibilities) or to try, at some possible danger to ourselves, to do something about it (extension of its possibilities), we also have alternative ways of cognizing it, in particular of cognizing it with respect to its felt contradictions.

The first of these cognitive modes is called *interpretive thinking* (*Deuten*). This mode effectively takes things as they appear to be, that is, at face value. The world – or, more strictly speaking, the life situation – is understood as being as it ought to be and the felt contradictions are treated as personal problems to be resolved within the sphere of one's own experience. It is easy to see how this relates to the mere utilization of available action possibilities, and also to repression as the most efficient means of handling the inevitable contradictions between one's own and the dominant interests.

If there are problems with this mode of thinking, it is not because it is 'wrong' in the sense of being an untrue representation of reality. Indeed, it is characterized by the correctness with which it grasps the immediate, superficial demands of the life situation. The problem is rather that it treats its limited understanding of the world as a complete, or completely representative, understanding of the world. It fails to make the distinction between what in other contexts are called essence and appearance. It fails to see that things might be otherwise than they are. The future is a simple continuation of the present and the past. It represents static, as opposed to developmental, thinking. Being arrested in the immediately given, it lacks the epistemic distance spoken of earlier as so vital to the assessment of relations among conditions and interests and to the eventual extension of action possibilities (and therefore also of the quality of life).

Interpretive thinking is a highly personalized mode of thinking, failing as it does to grasp the historical and societal interconnectedness of the whole, and thus also to grasp the self as an instance of the generalized other. It therefore also lacks a sense of subjectivity as intersubjectivity. It leads to the instrumentalization of others, and thus to restrictive action potence.

The opposite of interpretive thinking is *comprehensive thinking* (*Begreifen*). This is the mode of thought associated with extending possibilities for action. It makes use of epistemic distance to assess reality. It sees that things are often other than they appear to be, that conditions have been different in the past and can be different in the future from what they are in the present. It is the kind of thinking required for generalized action potence, and thus also for effective collective action aimed at the improvement of the general quality of life. While comprehensive thinking is necessary for generalized action potence, it is not sufficient in itself to overcome the contradictions standing in the way of the extension of personal action potence.

As with the two kinds of action potence, the two modes of cognition do not characterize people so much as particular thought-action patterns. That is to say, they are analytic categories that can assist us in identifying for ourselves and others particular directions in thought together with their consequences. In practice they are not mutually exclusive. Just as extension of possibilities is itself an extension of the utilization of possibilities, comprehensive thinking is an extension of interpretive thinking; the former cannot develop without prior development of the latter. Moreover, comprehensive thinking does not replace interpretive thinking; it rather incorporates and expands it. For any particular individual at any particular time, the distinction represents a choice, a real pair of alternatives. As Holzkamp observes: 'There is absolutely no degree of societal repression or personal developmental handicap that could justify the exclusion of any individual from the possibility of comprehensive thinking' (1983: 396). As possibilities, one is as generally available as the other. Probabilities, however, may vary greatly.

From a general, societal point of view – and therefore from a personal one as well, owing to their essential identity – there exists a distinct necessity in the long run for comprehensive thinking. Generalized action potence is impossible without it. But given the risks associated with generalized action potence and thus also with comprehensive thinking, it is at first hard to see what would move a person from interpretive to comprehensive thinking. The former is altogether less demanding, as well as being relatively risk-free. Ensconced in interpretive thinking, why should anyone want to move? The answer is found in our conception of the unconscious. It is well known that what has been repressed does not remain completely unnoticed. The reality of the self-hostility that repression seeks to hide remains only relatively hidden for most of us, thus the continued need for psychotherapy or other palliatives. We are constantly surrounded by reminders that urge the repressed contradictions into consciousness. We must constantly deal with doubts about the accommodations we make to the dominant powers for short-term benefits. The functionality, in short, of the restrictive, interpretive modes and the repression into the unconscious that they require are limited. And there is only one way of effectively dealing with this limitation, which is to take the risky route towards comprehensive thinking and generalized action potence.

EMOTION

The question of moving from one mode of cognition to another raises the larger one of motivation, and especially of emotion. We have learned that emotion essentially constitutes the subjective assessment of the individual's overall situation. We can expect that, in relation to generalized action potence, that is exactly how it is understood and used. As such, it complements comprehensive thinking in the formulation of subjective grounds for actions that extend possibilities and improve the quality of life. We know, however, that in bourgeois society this state is not uncomplicated by risks stemming from the imbalance of power and dominance and the corresponding differences in interests. The urgent question for us then concerns the distortions of emotion that occur in the restrictive situation.

The most important characteristic of emotion under restrictive action potence is its dissociation from cognition. If I am accommodating demands in my life situation that are, in fact, contrary to my (and the general) interest, my emotions as subjective assessment of that situation will be telling me things that I basically don't want to know, as, for example, about the contradictions between my own and the dominant interests that I am denying by confining my cognition to interpretive thinking. In such a circumstance, reading my emotions correctly can be decidedly dangerous. It is interesting to note how this dissociation is re-inforced by ideology, which is in turn reinforced by most psychological theories (as ideological instruments) that tell us that emotion and cognition are separate and that the former has to be kept under control in order not to interfere with the effective functioning of the latter. Emotion is treated, in short, not as an important informative factor but as an irrational disturbing one.

Corresponding to this dissociation of emotion and cognition is the personal internalization of emotion. It comes to be treated as a purely subjective state, often thought of as caused by an autonomic nervous system gone out of control. The obvious treatment, therefore, is not directed at the life situation of the individual but at the individual's person. Anxiety, for instance, which forms the inevitable background for the restrictive mode, is treated by administering tran-quillizing drugs or by otherwise therapeutically 'defusing' it. This seems reason-able because, owing to the repression that must accompany interpretive thinking, there really is no obvious cause; anxiety under these circumstances seems truly incomprehensible and the individual is genuinely helpless in the face of it. Treatments like the administration of tranquillizing drugs are thus obviously functional, not just for the dominant forces in society, but also subjectively for the individual who is thus made better able to continue in his or her commitment to interpretive thinking and restrictive action potence, even if, in fact, it con-stitutes a form of ideologically safe self-deception.

Effects of restrictive emotionality on interpersonal relations are especially noteworthy. Owing to the fact that restrictive action potence casts others into the role of instruments, it is not surprising that emotion plays a stellar function here. Emotions effectively become 'bargaining chips' in our compromising, compensatory dealings with others: 'If you give me affection, I'll give some in return; if you don't, I'll be sad and you'll feel guilty', etc. Emotional manipulation and blackmail become especially characteristic of close relationships, with all the agonizing results that become trivialized in cheap television melodrama, which either distracts us from our own agonies or consoles us with the assurance that we are not alone.

MOTIVATION

Motivation is the subjective emotional assessment of the life situation extended to the guidance of action on the basis of outcomes anticipated as meeting individual and generalized needs, that is, as serving the genuine interests of self and others. It should be obvious that with the restrictive distortions in emotion, motivation cannot fully function in this way.

> The motivation problematic of restrictive action potence within the interpretive framework of interiorized emotionality, etc. can be characterized as a situation that is both contradictory and ambivalent. On the one hand, from what on the surface appears to the individual as the functionality of his or her arrangement with the dominant forces, it would seem that the demands placed on action by the latter would serve his or her own interests and could therefore be responded to in a subjectively motivated fashion. On the other hand, even in the context of interpretive personalization, the actual compulsory character of the demands must be felt in individual experience. Here the motivation of the individual is not only displaced, but emotional impulses may be brought to the foreground that could place the whole arrangement in question, giving rise to an awareness of the danger stemming from the sanctions this would provoke among the dominant forces, should these impulses be translated into action.
>
> (Holzkamp 1983: 412)

From the point of view of restrictive action potence, the only resolution of the ambivalence is increased personalization, which, in this case, means internalization of the external compulsion as one's own. True motivation, which is the natural accompaniment of generalized action potence and comprehensive thinking in the service of the actual interests of individuals and society at large, is *replaced by internalized external compulsion*. It is, therefore, not surprising that people operating predominantly in the restrictive mode appear to have the constant need of *being motivated* through incentives, etc. It is also interesting to note that the 'social' motivational research conducted by psychologists in this century, failing to make the distinction we are making here, has focused heavily on external compulsion and its internalization, as if that exhausted the topic.

DEVELOPMENT OF INDIVIDUAL SUBJECTIVITY

Except for those born with distinct physical defects or damage, human infants come into this world biologically prepared for societal existence. Following birth, biological development continues and any full account of psychological development must take this into consideration. Our concern here, however, is with the development of subjectivity – or, more specifically, of personal action potence – and that is, given the necessary biological preparation, a predominantly societal process. Our main concern, then, is with the development of the individual's *societal nature*. This is obviously a complex affair, of which the Critical Psychologists give a more detailed account than we can recount here. We shall have to confine ourselves, therefore, to a summary of some of its major features, emphasizing its dependence on societal relations and indicating some of the points at which the crucial division between generalized and restrictive action potence can occur, that is, where the distortions of what would otherwise be the norm are likely to take place.

The basic task of the child in development can be described as the achievement of personal exercise of control over the conditions relevant to the satisfaction of its own needs, needs which, of course, it shares with all other humans. Given that the infant is specifically human with respect to its needs and that such needs are only met in ways characteristic of human subjects in society, we can assume that the child's development will be driven by a subjective necessity – not at first conscious or reflective – to increase control over conditions, reduce anxiety, improve the quality of life, and reduce helplessness through the realization of societal possibilities. The question then is how the helpless, dependent infant becomes an action-potent grown-up.

Generally speaking, there are three fundamental goals that must be achieved as prerequisites to full action potence. The infant must gain some kind of competence with the objects around it; it must appropriate and generalize the meanings that form the basis of societal existence; and it must overcome immediacy in favour of a mediated relation to the world. These goals are accomplished only in societal contexts. The first of these contexts is domestic and is provided by the family or other immediate care-givers. What develops there in terms of meanings, skills, grounds for action, etc., must then be generalized from the domestic to the broader societal context.

In the acquisition of competence with objects several important developments can be identified. The initial stages of dealing with things by looking, reaching, and manipulating are clearly unmediated, but soon become for the child part of a cooperative relationship with the care-giver. It is in this cooperative relationship that the child learns that things are not merely usable but useful. A spoon, for example, may first be treated as something that can be grasped, banged against other things, put into the mouth, etc. The child eventually learns that the spoon is held in a particular way and that it serves mainly for conveying food from a dish to the mouth. This particular use of a spoon is, of course, the societal meaning that is appropriated by the child in the course of this transition. Part of the meaning of a spoon is that it is *made for a particular use*. The child's later making of things is an extension of this kind of meaning and is ultimately generalized into making for others. The child draws a picture or builds something with blocks for the parent, who then responds approvingly and appropriately to the object portrayed or constructed. The child here is already participating in the production of social meanings and thus also in societal production. The child knows that things have meanings, that they are made, that they are made not only for oneself but for others, just as other objects meaningful for the child are made by others (as when the care-giver bakes the child's favourite cake). The development of language is, of course, central to this process. It all constitutes a growing up *in* as well as *into* societal relations, and at the domestic stage is effectively a development not merely of the child but of the child/care-giver coordination.

Learned meanings of objects obviously lead the child to a greater control over its own conditions. This occurs first in the domestic sphere, but then generalizes to the world at large. Playing with other children and experiencing them in their own homes help the child to generalize its own meanings and competencies. This begins to take place in a more intense and formal way with the onset of school-age.

The appropriation and generalization of societal meanings by the child lead also to a more complexly mediated relation to the world. It is here that grounds for action develop to replace direct determination by the environment, and the child develops the epistemic distance that allows it to assess its own relation to the world and the possibilities that the latter offers, and then finally to extend these possibilities.

It is not difficult to see how the process, which as sketched here would lead naturally to generalized action potence and comprehensive thinking, can be short-circuited. Since the entire process is a societal one, it depends as much, or more, on the care-givers and others around the child as, or than, it does on the child itself. The appropriation of meanings can be stifled by sheer neglect on the part of the care-giver. The development of intersubjectivity can be distorted by the care-giver's instrumentalization of his or her relations with the child or by encouraging the child to instrumentalize others. The development of comprehensive thinking can be retarded by authoritarianism on the part of the care-giver. These are only some of the more obvious ways in which the development of action potence, and thus subjectivity, can be diverted into the restrictive modes of emotionality, motivation, and cognition.

The significant point for us is that the developmental process is itself an essentially societal process. Other people are not merely important as features of the child's environment. They form the child's societal context and represent for it the larger context into which the child must grow. The development of the individual child is thus linked in an essential way to the development of society itself.

Part IV

Towards practice

Chapter 8

Methodological implications

How does this restructuring of the psychological categories and the consequent rethinking of individual subjectivity affect the way that one does psychology? Surely a conceptual reconstitution of the discipline as radical as the one we have described must have equally radical implications for practice in research and applied areas. We shall examine some of these methodological implications here.

As with the conceptual side of the psychological enterprise, we must begin with a critique of current method as a basis for its reconstruction along lines consistent with our theoretical conclusions. An important consideration will naturally be to develop methods that come closer to illuminating the actual problems of human subjectivity. As we shall see, this will lead us directly back to the question of relevance with which we began in Chapter 1.

CURRENT RESEARCH PRACTICE

The day-to-day practice of psychological researchers in mainstream, bourgeois psychology[1] is governed by what the German Critical Psychologists call the 'variable-model'.[2] Under this model, as we have already noted in Chapter 3, the subject matter of psychology is conceived of as a universe of actually or potentially measurable variables, the relations among which form the basis for all the discipline's scientific propositions and laws. The method by which such relations are established is the statistical method. This method is constituted by three broad aspects: measurement, analysis, and inference. Fundamentally, the same methods, and therefore also the same assumptions of the variable-model, are adopted both by psychologists who practise experimental psychology and by those engaged in psychometrics. The two types of research have the same historical roots and are concerned with effectively the same end, namely to produce statistical laws that allow the prediction of the behaviour of individuals or groups.

The use of measurement in connection with human affairs is not new. Its use by Theodor Fechner in his founding of psychophysics in the mid-nineteenth century is well known to students of psychology. Modern statistical applications of measurement, however, are usually considered to have been initiated by Adolphe Quételet in the first half of the nineteenth century, although others, especially Auguste Comte, had spoken of the possibility even earlier. Francis Galton applied measurement and statistical analysis to the specifically psychological question of intelligence in the 1880s. The conversion of Galton's psychometric method into a method for comparing groups of school pupils for the purpose of assessing the effectiveness of educational practices was accomplished by W. H. Winch in 1908 (Danziger 1990). This was the first application of 'experimental design', in its twentieth-century statistical sense, to a psychological question. Virtually all the more sophisticated measurement, analytic, and inferential techniques we identify with today's scientific psychology are elaborations of the techniques developed by Galton and Winch.[3]

The method's ontological assumptions are essentially identical to those enunciated by classical empiricism, and perpetuated by positivism and the various brands of neo-positivism that have been so influential in twentieth-century psychology. The world is assumed to be a composite of elements (variables) that are associated in differing ways and degrees. Moreover, like classical empiricism and positivism, the assumptions include (at least implicitly) a Cartesian dualism of subject and object. At the heart of this dualism is an absolute metaphysical separation of the knowing subject and the world it is supposed to know. Once separated, the problem is to bring them back together in such a way as to make sense out of the ways in which we seem to know our world. Here is not the place to recount the history of this highly problematic position; we need only see how it is reflected in the mainstream bourgeois psychology of this century. This has been to treat the world of objects (that is, objects of knowledge or other subjective process) as a collection of discrete *independent variables* that combine with each other in additive fashion to form the complexity of what is called the stimulus environment. The subject, by contrast, has been conceptualized as a similarly additive and complex collection of discrete *dependent variables*. The solution for bringing these together in our theories has been provided by the straight line that best fits a bivariate plot of data with the independent variable ranged on the abscissa and the dependent variable on the ordinate. The method for fitting this line is regression analysis, of which, as already indicated, virtually all research methods of analysis and inference are direct derivatives, and which particular research arrangements are designed to accommodate.

The inferential side of the variable-model methodology is not unproblematic. In cases where the independent and dependent variables are totally unrelated (noting that we must already violate the model in claiming to know this), their empirical measures will tend to show at least some degree of co-variation, that is, the regression line relating them will have a non-zero slope. This is said to be due to chance. On the other hand, when the variables can be presumed to be really related, the co-variation will tend not to be perfect. This is also ascribed, at least partly, to chance. Chance, or probability, then, plays a significant role in the procedure. Indeed, its role is essential, because the testing of hypotheses about the relationship between independent and dependent variables is always a comparison of actual results with those that would theoretically be obtained by chance alone. Sampling distributions of test statistics like t, F, and r, correspondingly, describe how these statistics distribute themselves theoretically under conditions of chance alone.

This creates a curious epistemic problem: the only hypothesis that can actually be tested in this procedure is the one that says the relationship is due to chance alone, the so-called 'null hypothesis', and the conclusion allowed by the test is only a negative one. That is, the only conclusion that can be drawn logically from a statistical test is that the null hypothesis is false. The awkwardness of the situation is further compounded by the fact that the conclusion itself can only be drawn with a 'degree of probability'. In short, there is little about the internal logic of the method that allows us to say anything definite and positive about anything.[4]

Psychologists do, however, proceed to make positive declarations on the basis of experimental evidence, but these must always be understood as separated from 'reality' (whatever that may mean for the variable-model) by several layers of uncertainty built into our methods and their underlying assumptions. Whether or not in making their knowledge claims particular psychologists are appropriately cautious about this does not change the underlying ontological framework of the variable-model that portrays a world of elements related to one another in probabilistic ways.

As Holzkamp (1983: 43) points out, the problem with all this from a Critical Psychological point of view is what it does to the human subject, that is, how it falls short of the ways in which we actually experience our lives. The subject is reduced to variables mechanically related by mathematical formulas to other variables. The human subject is no longer distinguishable in principle from other organisms (or any other collection of variables, for that matter) and is rendered utterly ahistorical, not to mention isolated and unsocietal. The variable model, in short, is constitutionally incapable of producing on its own the kind of understanding of the human subject that we have been attempting to develop in the preceding chapters.

THE PROBLEM OF OBJECTIVITY

An aspect of variable-model method universally acknowledged as crucial is its *objectivity*. There are several good reasons for the centrality of this concern. Not the least of these is that the method is based on the measurement of variables. With respect to environment (dependent variables), this seems completely unproblematic. If we are going to talk sensibly about the situation of an individual, we must be able to describe that situation in a way that distinguishes it on its own terms from other possible situations, and these differences are frequently ones of quantity. Objectivity here is equivalent simply to reliable description.

Things become somewhat more complicated, however, on the side of the subject (dependent variables). If it is a particular response or response pattern that interests us (we might even be so bold as to call it an 'action'), there is little difficulty. But what about the way a person *feels* about a situation? This is automatically ruled out by our commitment to measurement unless we can find some way of getting the person to express the feeling, as on, for example, a questionnaire. But what enters our equation then is not the subject's experience but a measurable response presumed to relate in some one-to-one fashion with a feeling. In principle, this need not be a problem. It is true that I do not feel your feelings and therefore depend on some indication from you to know about them. The Critical Psychological position developed in the preceding chapters would resolve the apparent problems in terms of the close relationship between public and private based on the societal nature of shared meanings.

But there *is* a problem here that has been known for quite a long time, and ignored by many for just as long. A classical example of this problem arose in Alfred Binet's observations on the two-point stimulation experiment. The experimenter touches the skin of the subject with a compass-like device on which the two points can be presented as one or two with varying degrees of separation. The subject is asked to report whether one or two points are felt. The obvious aim is to measure the two-point discrimination threshold. Nothing, it appears, could be simpler than translating accurately the feeling of the subject into a verbal response of either 'one' or 'two'. But Binet did not find it to be a simple matter at all.

> The first suggestion of what might be going on was provided by his [Binet's] fifteen-year-old daughter, Madeleine, whom he had put through a number of these experiments, only to find the usual 'practice' effects. 'I knew better this time what the sensations meant,' she told him after a later session. 'When a sensation was a little "big", I thought there must be two points, because it was too thick for one.' What Madeleine had picked up was the rather elastic meaning of the category 'two' that had to be employed in this situation. Fortunately, her father had no particular stake in the psychophysical methods pioneered by his German rivals and decided to pursue the matter. He extended the investigation to adult subjects, permitting them to report freely on their experiences. Under these conditions Fechner's neat binary scheme of *either one or two* disintegrated. Subjects reported sensations between oneness and twoness – 'broad', 'thick', and 'dumbbell-shaped' sensations that could be categorized as 'one' or 'two', depending on the subject's interpretation of the schema that the experimenter wished to be applied.
>
> (Danziger 1990: 139)

Thus, already under extremely simple circumstances, a complexity can be shown to intervene between 'input' and 'output' that is completely missed or distorted by the reduction of our concern to the mere correlation of measurable variables. One problem is that, in order to maintain the objectivity required by the variable-model, the dependent variable must be pre-defined by the experimenter. As the example of Binet's daughter demonstrates, this had the result of utterly obscuring the underlying process or experience. To get at these, Madeleine had to define the response herself. Only in this way was her father able to gain access to her experience through shared meanings. The problem only multiplies in complexity as we move on to subjectively more significant events like those that make up our situations in our workplaces or in our families.

REDUCTION TO IMMEDIACY

The standard 'solution' to problems of subjectivity has been for psychologists to restrict their concern exclusively to relations among pre-defined variables, that is, to retreat still further into the fortress of the variable-model, thus creating the well-known problem of the 'black box', which amounts simply to ignoring all the messiness between independent and dependent variables. It must be acknowledged that not all mainstream psychologists have been happy with this patently mechanical treatment of psychological process. This unhappiness has been the basis for much discussion about 'intervening variables' and 'hypothetical constructs'. The problem of subjectivity, however, does not go away so easily. Owing to our commitment to the variable model, we have continued to think of these intervening events themselves *as variables* with exactly the same properties as those we called independent and dependent. The result of this has been that intervening variables have been reduced to pure theoretical abstractions (for example, personality traits) that figure mathematically (for example, as scores on a questionnaire) in the equation as additional independent variables, thus improving overall co-variation. The information thus gained is, as A. N. Leontyev put it, no more significant than learning that 'footprints will be clearly imprinted in soft, wet ground, but not in dry, parched ground' or that 'a hungry animal and a satiated animal will react differently to a food stimulus, and a football fan will respond quite differently to a final score than will someone with no interest in the game' (1981: 43). The intervening events, the acknowledgement of which seemed to hold some theoretical promise, thus become reduced to measurable external events, that is, to merely additional independent variables. The historical, societal, experiencing subject once more succumbs to the demands of the variable-model.

The reduction involved here is a reflection of what Leontyev called the 'postulate of immediacy' (1981: 42). Whatever the subject does, whether measurable or not, is seen simply as the 'effect' of external conditions, conditions that are either naturally occurring or determined by someone else.

The subject matter of such a theoretical [methodological] conception is reduced to a short-circuited connection between 'conditions' and 'activities' by excluding the mediational levels of 'meaning' and 'grounds for action'. These 'conditions' cannot be societal 'life conditions' and therefore cannot be understood as human possibilities for action. That which makes actions human, namely the subjectively grounded possibility relation, and thus also consciousness as conscious 'relating-to', along with all the accompanying specifics of the functional aspects of human action potence, thus remain outside the limits of consideration.

(Holzkamp 1983: 525)

In short, every important aspect of subjectivity as we have outlined it in the preceding chapter is summarily excluded from scientific consideration by the methods of mainstream psychology.

Not only is the human subject, whose most important characteristic is the capacity to create conditions, methodologically de-subjectified into a non-subject who merely reacts to conditions: to the extent that human subjectivity is simultaneously intersubjectivity, it, too, is eliminated by these methods. The subject–experimenter relationship, for example, is a very peculiar one in the variable-model. It is one in which the experimenter is ideally invisible. Where visibility cannot be avoided, the experimenter is standardized so as to approximate a piece of equipment. A paradoxical result of this is that, under conditions that are supposed to neutralize subjectivity, it is really only the subjectivity of the experimenter that can be controlled successfully in an experiment. Despite the most rigorous measures, the subject always remains to some extent a 'free agent'. As a result, subjects are known to be occasionally uncooperative. They therefore often 'screw up' experiments and their data must be discarded.

A recognition of this problem has led to the development of an entire body of research on the 'social psychology of experiments' (Alcock *et al.* 1988: 34–36). The general result of this work has been to produce more refined experimental designs (for example, the 'double-blind' procedure and techniques for assessing and controlling 'demand effects') in order to gain greater compliance from the subjects. Some researchers have gone so far as to identify potentially distorting roles ('faithful', 'cooperative', 'negative', and 'apprehensive') that subjects appear to adopt in an experiment (Weber and Cook 1972). Although deception of subjects is looked upon with increasingly less favour nowadays, it continues to be used, often in subtler forms, as a way of combating deception of the experimenter by the subject (Holzkamp 1983: 527, 567). The question we must be asking ourselves is why all this deception and exercise of artificial control are necessary. We shall return to this.

RESEARCH AS THE REPRODUCTION OF BOURGEOIS RELATIONS

The total reduction to immediacy demanded by the variable-model represents a kind of 'worst-case scenario' of the tendency created by bourgeois society's imbalance of power and interests to deny mediacy and to emphasize utilization over expansion, interpretation over comprehension, and restrictive over generalized action potence. The method simply mimics actual bourgeois societal relations of dominance. This structural partisanship is built into psychology's understanding of its subject matter and its corresponding methods.

A standard objection to such an assessment has been that scientific methods are ideologically neutral, that is, are strictly objective and do not favour one set of values or interests over another. A defender of this objection may point to work on sensory thresholds or on perceptual-motor coordination and challenge anyone to find ideology there. This defence is a good one: there is nothing obviously ideological about a sensory threshold. The information is important for many unassailably scientific, theoretical, and practical reasons, none of which favours dominant interests. Moreover, this information can only be obtained under highly controlled conditions that demand absolute cooperation (one could even say 'submission') of the subject. This is not unlike what we ought to expect of a good medical or optometrical examination. So there *is* a case to be made for the methods we have critically described, a case that is essentially free of ideological considerations.

This does not alter our concerns, however, when it comes to questions of human activity that go beyond basic psychophysiological processes, questions that touch the specifically human qualities of psychical functioning. When it comes, for example, to what Wundt called the 'higher mental processes' (in which we would now include emotion, learning, motivation, etc., in their specifically *human*, subjective aspect) the method remains fundamentally and irreparably eliminative and distorting. Moreover, the relationship between this elimination and distortion and the bourgeois relations of production cannot be accidental: the method is thoroughly and inescapably ideological and partisan.

What about the attitude of the psychologist? Surely these methods are applied daily by politically progressive women and men, who on no account would openly support bourgeois suppression. This changes nothing: a method based on immediacy can do nothing other than exclude the mediated nature of human experience that forms the very foundation for the societal nature and subjectivity of individuals, no matter what private attitudes are held by the experimenter. Speaking of progressive scientific intentions of psychologists, Holzkamp writes:

> As soon as one operationalizes these aims for the purpose of empirically realizing them by using traditional experimental-statistical procedures, the question reduces itself necessarily to the form: 'Under what conditions do people do this or that?' Thus: 'Under what conditions do people organize trade union activities, develop class consciousness, take part in socialist causes, arrive at an independent apprehension of their own interests, join forces for common purposes?' Here the progressively intended promotion of collective self-determination by individuals gets cancelled out by directing the question at the externally set conditions for self-determination. What can never be meant here (owing to the structure of the methodological procedure) are the conditions that individuals create for themselves in order to improve their possibilities in life, but rather always and only the conditions that 'someone' sets for them, where the 'someone' implies not a generalized version of the subject's point of view but an implicit generalization of the standpoint of those who set the conditions 'for them'. . . . The progressive viewpoint of the psychologist is not sufficient: what is needed is the right psychology, one that

does not constantly sabotage progressive intentions by the structure of its method.

(Holzkamp 1983: 530–531)

The methods of mainstream, bourgeois psychology[5] are tailor-made for restrictive action potence and all that implies. Their structure allows nothing else. It is therefore not surprising that emotion always appears as something internal, separated from and basically a threat to cognition and action. It is not surprising that cognition always appears in its interpretive, not its comprehensive, form. It is not surprising that motivation always appears as internalized compulsion. The universalization of the restrictive mode of relating to the world is the necessary consequence of experimental-statistical methodology.

NEED OBJECTIVITY BE SACRIFICED?

Mainstream, bourgeois psychology found itself faced with an old and serious problem. It appears to have been obvious to the founders of our scientific discipline – people like Wundt and James – that the subject matter of psychology was some form of 'mental life' (James) or 'higher mental processes' (Wundt), that is, that the 'mental' ought to be the focus of scientific psychological attention. There were many attempts in the second half of the nineteenth century to define the 'mental' as opposed to the physical: for Wundt it depended on whether the experience was mediate or immediate; for Brentano it was a matter of the intentionality of the mental. By 1913 (the year of J.B. Watson's behaviourist manifesto) it was becoming obvious to many (or so they thought) that however one defined the 'mental' it remained subjective in a way that prevented its being susceptible to 'really scientific' investigation. Science was, of course, understood as essentially characterized by the objectivity of its methods and of its knowledge claims. The end result, one that dominated scientific psychological thinking for most of this century, was the sacrifice of the 'subjective' for a subject matter that was unequivocally objective. Only this, it seemed, would yield a psychology that commanded respect in the scientific community.

The only thing that really divided scientific psychologists by the 1930s was whether or not the mental language should be retained. It is well known that Watson and Skinner were adamant in their rejection of it; moderates like Carr and Woodworth found nothing wrong with retaining the language, while being always careful to define it objectively. For example, in 1925 Carr still described psychology as 'the study of mental activity', but was quick to explain that by this he meant 'adaptive or adjustive behavior' (Carr 1925: 1). By contrast, Watson, being accustomed to 'calling a spade a spade', insisted on a tidier, more Spartan approach (cf. Watson 1930).

By the 1960s, when behaviourism was beginning to fall out of favour, many psychologists were deserting the mainstream in order to reassert the importance of subjectivity. They adopted various labels for themselves, such as 'humanistic', 'phenomenological', and 'existential'. The resonance among students and younger psychologists of the time was great. We shall not linger here over the rise and fall of these alternative psychologies, nor over their likely important role in precipitating and reinforcing the so-called cognitive revolution of the 1970s. What is important for our present purposes is that the general tendency they represented simply inverted the priority of the objective over the subjective. In short, they accepted the mainstream premise that the two opposed each other and that a choice had to be made. But science was still identified with objectivity. Even this was accepted by many of the rebels, who then simply rejected the 'scientific model' for psychology.

The culprit here is a mode of thinking mentioned earlier in this chapter and called 'Cartesian' after René Descartes, who provided us with one of its clearest articulations, though it is a mode of thinking that dominated Western thought well before Descartes and continues to dominate it, often even among those who regard themselves as anti-Cartesian. This mode of thinking is characterized by the view that objects are defined exclusively in and of themselves and thus exist entirely independently of all other things. This includes opposites or seemingly opposing entities. The most important for us are mind and body. They are conceived as primordially separate entities that just happen to coexist in human beings. Given that they are entirely separate, Descartes was forced to imagine that they were related through causal effects of one upon the other. With this mind–body distinction goes a host of related distinctions: subject–object, internal–external, private–public, and subjectivity–objectivity.

Science had an important impact on this distinction. Since the earliest successes of modern science were achieved through the application of mathematics (as in geometry and the early physics of bodies in motion), there developed a close association between science and measurement. Indeed for many, if not most, scientists of the last 400 years the two have been identified. For example, for Hume 'the only objects of the abstract science or of demonstration are quantity and number, and . . . all attempts to extend this more perfect species of knowledge beyond these bounds are mere sophistry and illusion' (1777/1966: 182).[6] If one proceeds to the apparent logical implication, reality (or whatever of reality is worth knowing) was that which was treated by science, and we end up with the claim ascribed to Lord Kelvin that 'if it cannot be measured, it does not exist'.

One of the better known implications for a developing psychology was the division between 'primary' and 'secondary' qualities. The former were qualities like extension, size, and number. They were thought to be properties inhering in the object itself, that is, physical properties. They were measurable. Secondary qualities were those like tonal pitch, colour, and taste. These were considered to be qualities that the subject added to the object in its being perceived. They could not be measured. To the extent that secondary qualities were admitted, then, there was room for a psychology, but that it could be a *scientific* psychology was generally doubted. It was Kant's pronouncement on the matter in 1786 (1970:

Preface) that challenged many of the great figures of our discipline's history, such as Herbart and Fechner, to find ways of mathematizing mental events. The problem was and remains, however, that what they succeeded in measuring were external, objective events; the mental remained subjective and therefore out of reach and problematic.

There have been many attempts to overcome the Cartesian separation of subject and object. Some of the greatest names in the history of philosophy and psychology are associated with such attempts: Hobbes, Berkeley, Hegel, Mach, James, and Dewey, to name but a few. The 'solution' takes three distinct forms. Extreme materialists (e.g. Hobbes and modern 'eliminativists') seek to eliminate the split either by claiming to reduce the subjective exhaustively to the objective ('thought is really nothing but neural activity in the brain') or by denying that there is anything real enough to be reduced. Extreme idealists make the complementary reduction or elimination (e.g. Berkeley's *'esse* is *percipi'*, i.e. 'to be is to be perceived'). These prove, however, to be non-solutions. The extreme materialists are left unable to explain why, for example, we should ever have developed the illusion of subjectivity in the first place, and why, if it is merely an illusion, we should have developed such a rich vocabulary about subjective events. For most (all?) of us, our qualities of experience are just as real as the extension of the table we are touching. The extreme idealists, on the other hand, have difficulty dealing with the compellingness of our experience. Why are we afraid to be cut by the knife? To answer, as the idealist might, that we are afraid because we know that the experience of being cut will be followed by the experience of pain is not good enough, because it does not tell us why this *must* be the case, that is, why it is not experienced simply as one event followed by another but as pain *necessarily* following from the cut.

A third solution is found in the work of people like Hegel, Marx, James, Dewey, and many others who appear to hold otherwise very different views of the world. This rejection of Cartesianism argues that the subject and object *are* different from each other but that they are not completely separate because the subject is an evolutionary, historical, or developmental extension of the object itself. It begins and remains a part of the overall objective process. In the terms of dialectical logic, we must be able to see how the subject and object are 'identical' yet 'different' at the same time. Identity does not exclude difference or vice versa. What is required to make this a real solution to the problem is an account of the development of the subject from the object and of its function in the overall objective process. This is precisely what we have been outlining in the preceding chapters. Subjectivity emerges in an evolutionary process simultaneously with the societal mode of existence. As such, it occurs only in society, a fact that we have expressed as intersubjectivity: subjectivity *is* intersubjectivity:

> According to our categorial analyses, my own subjective standpoint is indeed the starting point for my experience of the world and of my self, but it is not an inevitable, self-sufficient finality. If I work through my immediate

experience in the historical-analytical way we have described, then I find that, for everyone, my standpoint as starting point of my experience is also the endpoint of a phylogenetic or societal-historical development, by which it became at once necessary and possible only as an aspect of the material, societal life-supporting process, as a characteristic of the conscious 'possibility relations' of individuals to societal relations through the general societal mediatedness of their existence. The standpoint of the subject is thus neither eliminated nor reduced by such a logical-historical reconstruction, but rather, in the process, I rediscover myself consciously and scientifically reflected in the very place in the societal context where I have in fact always stood: as an individual relating myself to the societal maintenance system through which my own existence is generalized and co-maintained, as I consciously relate to my subjective possibilities for action; this conscious 'ability to relate' representing a necessary, defining aspect of the material production and reproduction of societal life and thereby also of my own existence.

(Holzkamp 1983: 538)

The standpoint of subjectivity thus does not exclude objective conditions; rather, it *includes* them. What is excluded is simply the distorted account of our individual subjective relations to those conditions. Holzkamp argues that the outcome of the Critical Psychological analysis of categories itself is sufficient evidence (if we need any more than our everyday experience already provides) that we can arrive at objective knowledge about human subjectivity.

BUT CAN WE GENERALIZE?

Science requires objectivity, and we have shown how a science of the subject can be objective. Science also requires generalization. That a science of the individual subject can generalize should already be apparent from our analysis of individual subjectivity as an instance of the generalized other. It is necessary, however, to specify the problem of scientific generalization in a bit more detail, because the kind of generalization we are advocating is different in important ways from the kind usually sought by mainstream scientific methods in psychology.

The understanding of generalization that has become standard for mainstream psychology in this century is one that is closely linked to the abstract. According to a prominent psychological dictionary:

A concept requires both abstraction and generalization – the first to isolate the property, the second to recognize that it may be ascribed to several objects. But we distinguish a class concept or a general concept from an abstract concept, depending upon our desire to emphasize one or the other aspect of conceiving.

(English and English 1958: 105)

The authors stress that abstraction cannot occur without generalization since we cannot isolate a property without looking at a number of cases, and generalization obviously cannot occur without abstraction. The real distinction between the two, as the last sentence in the above quotation indicates, is simply the aspect of the process the particular psychologist wishes to emphasize. This is why statistical analysis is so important to psychological method: only that which a population of subjects has in common can be generalized, and that is the abstraction we call the arithmetic mean. The resulting laws of our science therefore attain generality by pertaining to means rather than to individual instances.

There are some obvious problems with this conceptualization of generalization, at least one of which we have already alluded to in other contexts. This problem is that it can only achieve its goal by sacrificing the concrete particulars of the individual instance. In the end, what becomes explained is the average behaviour, not that of a particular individual. Individual deviations – which are after all what will interest most of us as individuals – are eliminated very early in the analysis as 'error variance'. For a method that proclaims itself modern, empirical, and scientific, this procedure's flirtation with Platonism should be a monumental embarrassment to its practitioners.[7] It clearly appears to presume the existence of abstract, real universals that can be discovered with the aid of mathematics by penetrating the accidents of mere appearance.

A second problem – clearly related to the first and equally embarrassing for any conscientious scientist – is that the method is obviously aimed at establishing the lawfulness of nature, which it must presume at the outset. In short, the method is patently question-begging. This accounts for the fact that so many psychological 'laws' (such as those of reinforcement, discrimination, stimulus generalization, short- and long-term memory, impression formation, bystander effects, etc.) often strike the uninitiated as intuitively obvious: they *are* intuitively obvious! Despite their obviousness, such laws do not shed much light on individual cases. The uninitiated might be heard to say something like 'I *knew* that, but what about my problem?' This lack of relation to the individual instance is precisely what is felt as 'irrelevance'. Where irrelevance appears to be overcome, we tend to find a pattern characterized by two stages. First, there is an enormous research effort aimed at establishing the abstract regularities of a problem. Once this is completed and attention turns to applying the new knowledge to practice, such as in psychotherapy or counselling, a second stage must be initiated in which effective practices are established by empirical means, that is, by trying different techniques to find out which ones work. The embarrassment here is that the correct practice cannot be deduced from the laws discovered in the first phase, and this is because those laws pertain to the realm of the abstract, while the practice pertains to individual, concrete instances. It is built into our methods that the relationship between the abstract and concrete is a one-way street: we move easily from the concrete to the abstract, but return only by way of predictions that apply to populations, not to individuals.

One way in which this embarrassment has been avoided has been to create situations (as frequently seen in educational and other institutional settings) that are so devised as to eliminate concrete individual differences, thereby forcing individuals into the mould of the abstraction (recall the instance of the children in the bare room with only a lever to manipulate). Where we find application of this solution in education and industry, it is obvious that what the psychologist has gained concrete knowledge of is situations and how they can be used to control otherwise 'deviant' individuals. There is no evident knowledge of subjects as concrete individual cases.

What, then, is the alternative? For a start, it is important to note that the accepted understanding in psychology of generalization-as-abstraction is a relatively new invention in modern science. It arrived with the introduction of statistical analysis coupled with administrative needs to control collections of individuals (for a detailed account of this history, see Danziger 1990). There is an older understanding of scientific generalization, one that dominated German psychology in the late nineteenthth and first half of the twentieth century and is still found in the physical sciences. According to this older conception the 'typical case' is established through a combination of established empirical knowledge and theoretical understanding. This, it should be noted, is simply specifying the lawfulness that is presumed to exist and which therefore does not have to be established. Generalization then consists of working out the mediating factors that account for the deviations of concrete, individual instances. Generalization does not move from the concrete to the abstract, but from the abstract to the concrete: the equation of abstract and general is rejected from the outset (cf. Tolman 1991b). The ultimate aim of science is accordingly not to achieve the general by abstraction, but to start with the abstract and make it general by tying it back to the concrete.

This is an understanding that governed the work of Wundt and most of his younger German colleagues. A more recent and familiar articulation of it is found in the well-known article on the 'Aristotelian versus Galileian' modes of thought in biology and psychology (Lewin 1931). De Rivera (1976) links Lewin's conception to Ernst Cassirer's definition of scientific concept, which de Rivera summarizes as follows:

[A] scientific concept (actually, *any* concept) is not an abstraction of something that is substantially common to each of the cases to which the concept may be applied. Instead, each concept is a construction in its own right, a relational construction that is separate from each case, yet can generate each unique concrete instance.

(de Rivera 1976: 16–17)

The categorial reconstruction of psychology that we have outlined in the preceding chapters is precisely such a 'relational construction' that is prepared to 'generate each unique concrete instance' and thus achieve generality. In our own case, the only real test of generality is the extent to which our abstractions (such as 'action possibility', 'subjective situation', and 'action potence') illuminate the experience of concretely, societally situated persons. Understood in this way, generality, strictly speaking, is not the ability to move conceptually from the concrete to the abstract (the exclusive understanding associated with the variable model), nor is it simply the reverse of this; rather, it represents an ability to move equally readily from one to the other. To have generality means that we understand the linkage between the abstract and the concrete. It should now be obvious that this cannot be achieved by our current mainstream methods of measurement and statistical analysis.

TOWARDS THEORETICAL DETERMINACY

We now have what Holzkamp believes are the two major methodological requirements for resolving the problem of theoretical indeterminacy as it was described in Chapter 4. These are (1) a framework within which we can determine what is relevant or essential and (2) a concrete understanding of scientific generalization.

At the biological level of existence, the functional-historical method provided a categorial framework for judging relevance. From the results of this method described in Chapter 5 it can be seen, for example, that a theory of animal emotion that treated its manifestations solely in terms of underlying physiological mechanisms could well prove to be factually correct, but in the absence of an appropriate methodological framework it would likely overlook the assessment function, which is the evolutionarily relevant aspect of emotion for the life of the individual animal as well as of its species. Moreover, the type of theory developed within our categorial framework cannot be one that seeks abstract universality. It must be able to explain individual cases in which the assessment function fails or becomes distorted, or the different ways in which the function may be achieved by different species. A theory that achieves these ends will surely be preferred to one that is merely factually correct and abstractly universal.

At the societal level of existence the framework of relevance and essentiality is provided by categories such as action potence, subjective situation, and possibility relationship. Theories of alteration of response frequency through reinforcement are certainly factually correct, but they do nothing to elucidate the complexities and exigencies of a societally situated individual human life. Theories of particular psychological processes that both reflect relevance and generalize to individual cases have not been described in any great detail in this book, but indications of such theories (e.g. of the unconscious, emotion, motivation, and cognition) have been sketched in the previous chapter. What is important at this point is to see that the kind of theory that the German Critical Psychologists are aiming for is a different kind of theory, one that cannot be judged by the criteria of mainstream psychology (such as statistical reliability). It can only be judged by the degree to which it reflects relevance and essentiality as determined by a broadly evolutionary/historical method such as has been described on the preceding pages and by the degree to which it illuminates experience and empowers the individual human subject.

HOW, THEN, DO WE PROCEED?

Let us begin by establishing the absolute prerequisite for any empirical research (or applied practice) from the point of view of the Critical Psychologists' reconstruction of categories. Recall that the principal focus of our concern is the subjective situation of the individual with its relationship to action potence, action possibilities, grounds for action, etc. In so far as these categories and the theoretical structure that they constitute illuminate the individual subjective situation, the first person to be affected will be the researcher-as-subject who has appropriated and understood this structure. But both the objectivity and the generality that our research aims for are only to be found in *intersubjectivity*. The intersubjectivity that we are seeking, however, is not the one that we all necessarily share owing to our common societal existence; it is one focused on the individual subjectivities of the sharing individuals and on subjectivity generally. For that reason, we must identify a special form of intersubjectivity, namely *metasubjectivity*.

The metasubjectivity required is one shared by the researcher and the person that mainstream psychology identifies as the 'subject'. (Considering the actual de-subjectifying nature of mainstream psychological research method, and in order to avoid confusion with our own use of the term 'subject', we shall call this person the 'other person', or simply 'other'.) The first significant and necessary generalization occurs, then, when the other person appropriates the theoretical structure that permits communication between him or her and the researcher. The relationship must be a truly communicative one, and this means assuring that the relevant concepts and methods are put into the hands of the other person. The knowledge that results from such a procedure is thus not merely knowledge *about* the other person, but knowledge *for* the other person.

An important corollary is that the problem investigated must also be a problem *for* the other person. This does not necessarily mean that the other person must come to the researcher with a complaint, but that the problem be understood by the person as a problem, the understanding of which is in his or her interest.

To readers steeped in current mainstream methods these prescriptions may seem odd indeed. We therefore need to be reminded that they are not at all new. Virtually all 'classical' German psychological research (and much of that elsewhere) was conducted under these or similar assumptions (for a critical and historical account of this, see Danziger 1990). Wundt served as Cattell's other and vice versa; Wertheimer was Köhler's other and vice versa; Marbe was Bühler's other and vice versa. In his work on memory, which is still regarded as valuable, Ebbinghaus was his own other, and the same is true of most of Stumpf's work on tonal perception. This was the approach with which experimental psychological research got its start, and which was only gradually displaced during the first half of this century by the statistical investigation of groups of 'naive' individuals. This was not, as is commonly believed, because the older method failed to produce objective, scientific knowledge, but because it failed to meet the new demands for the administrative management of de-subjectified groups of individuals.

A common objection, however, will be that a research method based on this 'classical' understanding of objectivity and generalization lacks the verifiability, falsifiability, and potential validity (in short, 'rigour') normally claimed for experimental-statistical methods. On the contrary. Such a method arguably enhances rigour. Considering that we are now working from the 'standpoint of the subject' and that the subject is (indeed, must be) a fully informed co-researcher, hypotheses about how our categories are mediated in his or her experience of the world are immediately subject to verification and/or falsification according to exactly the same canons of logic that govern all scientific inference. The difference is only that the test of the theory is now in the hands of the subject (experimenter, other person, co-experimenter), not left to the de-subjectified probabilities of statistical method. This means, among other things, that individual cases that do not conform to theoretical expectations must be taken seriously as at least partial falsification; they cannot be disposed of by identifying them as mere exceptions or instances of 'error variance'.

As in the generally accepted understandings of scientific verification and falsification, neither is absolute in the method proposed here; rather, instances of either are taken as playing an important role in the overall project of criticism, reinterpretation, and further development of existing theory. Now, since *all* instances, positive or negative, must be theoretically accommodated, it is hard to see how this could result in a loss of rigour at the level of immediate theory and practice. At the level of the theoretical categories rigour is distinctly increased, because, unlike the categories of traditional mainstream psychology, they are themselves grounded by an empirical-historical method that makes them equally subject to criticism, reinterpretation, and further development (cf. our earlier discussion of theoretical determinacy).

It is fair to ask about the criteria by which the validity of conclusions are judged. Recalling that our immediate focus of interest is the individual subjective situation and that this is the experiential side of action potence (which is finally aimed, both collectively and individually, at extending possibilities for action) it becomes plain that the actual, objective extension of such possibilities in individual cases is itself the ultimate criterion in practice of the correctness, if only tentative, of our theories.[8]

What about deception? It should be obvious that the method being proposed is one that, in principle, cannot involve deception of the other person, since that other person must be fully informed to the extent of being a genuine co-investigator. But what is to prevent this presumed co-investigator from deceiving the primary researcher? This possibility cannot be entirely eliminated, but certainly, given our requirement of metasubjectivity, it is markedly reduced by the fact that the usual causes and incentives for deception are removed and that the co-investigator has a personal interest in learning the actual state of affairs, because such knowledge has the potential of extending his or her real action possibilities and thus also his or her generalized action potence.

Looked at from this point of view, it can be seen how the borders between research and any other 'professional' practice necessarily fade. The situation we have outlined for empirical research is effectively the same, for instance, for psychotherapy and counselling. People seek therapy or counselling often just because they are caught in circumstances characterized by restrictive emotionality, cognition, and motivation, because they suffer the anxiety that accompanies restrictive action potence, and because they don't understand their situations and are not equipped with the skills to deal effectively with them. The client must be drawn into therapy or counselling just as the other person, the co-investigator, is drawn into the research process: a theoretical understanding must be appropriated, a state of metasubjectivity must be established, hypotheses must be tested in the real world, and action possibilities must be both subjectively and objectively extended. In short, both research and therapy are aimed finally at the *empowerment* of the subject (Dreier 1980, 1991). In this regard, Critical Psychology is not unlike psychoanalysis: both positions share common roots in 'classical' German philosophy and psychology (Holzkamp 1991b).

NON-SPECIFIC LEVELS OF HUMAN PSYCHOLOGICAL FUNCTIONING

We have said that the aim of Critical Psychological method is not to *exclude* objectivity – indeed, we must maintain and expand it – but to *include* subjectivity. In order to achieve the latter, it has become clear that traditional experimental-statistical methods are inappropriate. The overall picture must be tempered, however, by observing that the specifically human subjectivity that has been our focal concern, together with all its various features, is not the only aspect of human psychological functioning of potential concern. These functions are themselves dependent on lower-order or non-specific (in the sense of not distinguishing our species as human) functions, such as perceptual-motor coordination, that limit our possibilities yet do not represent societally imposed restrictions that can in principle be overcome. They belong, in Holzkamp's words, to

> the actual functional basis for human action potence, the prerequisites for the emergence of the conscious 'possibility relation', which are not at the total disposal of human beings, but whose lawful nature must be taken into consideration if humans are in fact to achieve the capability of disposing over external nature and their own natures in their long-term interests.
>
> (Holzkamp 1983: 575)

Aside from the mentioned perceptual-motor processes, we can name here virtually all the processes studied by physiological psychologists. It will be clear from the development of our categorial system at the functional-historical levels that there are also basic emotional, motivational, learning, and even proto-cognitive processes to be considered here. Such processes are necessarily excluded from the field of metasubjectivity in which the co-investigative methods we have discussed in this chapter apply.

CONCLUSION

The general methodological picture we are sketching, then, is one that accepts traditional, especially biologically based, psychological methods, but restricts them to the kinds of question for which they are competent. Even measurement and statistical analysis are not ruled out here. What is challenged are less the traditional methods than the claims psychologists make and unquestioningly accept about their universality. What we have tried to point out is that such claims force us to ignore what ought to be most important to us as human beings: our own subjectivity. If we are to take subjectivity seriously, then, as we have shown, we need a restructuring of our categorial framework to assist us in specifying the characteristics of subjectivity and its societal nature, and we need correspondingly to broaden our methodological base in order to devise methods of investigation and applied practice that respond adequately to the special nature of this subject matter. Only in this way can psychology produce the kind of knowledge that individual human beings need in order to expand their real possibilities for meaningful participation in the collective regulation of the conditions governing their own lives. Only in this way can psychology become genuinely *critical*.

Notes

1 IDEOLOGY, POWER, AND SUBJECTIVITY

1 A fuller account of the Ohnesorg incident can be found in the reports of *Der Spiegel*: 'Knüppel frei' 1967; 'Sehr heiss' 1967; and 'Urteil im Zwielicht' 1967.

2 A complete history of the Free University of Berlin can be found in Tent (1988).

3 On the student movement up to June 1967, see the report in *Der Spiegel*, 'Nein, nein, nein' 1967.

4 On the Critical University (*Kritische Universität*) see the report in *Der Spiegel*, 'Dr. crit.' 1967.

5 Critical Theory was an influential social philosophical position developed in the early 1930s by a group known as the Frankfurt School that included Theodor Adorno, Max Horkheimer, Herbert Marcuse, and others. This group was exiled to the United States during the Nazi period, some of them returning to Frankfurt to re-establish the School after the war. Since that time, Jürgen Habermas has become the position's most influential spokesperson. (See the pertinent entries in Abercrombie, Hill, and Turner 1988.)

6 Holzkamp's source is the speech made by Staeuble. For the published version, see Staeuble 1968.

7 The Emergency Law (*Notstandsgesetz*) was not directed only at student activities but at any and all activities that might be construed by the authorities as subversive. Organized opposition to it was widespread in the student movement, labour movement, and citizens' groups of all kinds.

8 The term 'sex-pol' refers to the sexual-political version of psychoanalysis developed by Wilhelm Reich in the 1930s. There was a revival of interest in Reich's thought among many student radicals of the 1960s and 1970s (e.g. Reich 1963).

9 This refers to the so-called *Mittelbau* which has no precise equivalent in British or North American universities. While it contained junior faculty who had not yet qualified for a professorial or other teaching rank, it also included scientific workers who, owing more to their particular function than to a lack of academic qualifications, would remain in that status for their entire careers.

10 When referring to the specific psychology developed in Berlin under this label it will be given initial capital letters in order to distinguish it from the general attempt to develop a psychology that is critical. This is consistent with current German usage.

11 See note 5.

2 PHILOSOPHICAL ASSUMPTIONS

1 No serious philosopher has advocated an empiricism quite so naive as the one that has implicitly informed so much of twentieth-century psychology, particularly in North America. It comes close at times, however, to 'British empiricism', especially the version argued by John Locke. A useful summary of this position is found in Hamlyn (1967). Some important criticisms of it are presented in the final three paragraphs of Hamlyn's article. The present account of naive empiricism is based on Holzkamp (1972: 80–81).

2 Kurt Danziger has described this understanding of science in the following way: 'The received view is based on a model of science that is reminiscent of the tale of Sleeping Beauty. The objects with which psychological science deals are all present in nature fully formed, and all the prince-investigator has to do is to find them and awaken them with the magic kiss of his research. . . . In the past the effects of a naive empiricism may have assigned an essentially passive role to investigators, as though they merely had to observe or register what went on outside them' (1990: 2).

3 The value-orientation of social science was a central feature of the social theory of Max Weber (see Freund 1969: 51–56). Although Weber's arguments have not gone unchallenged, few social thinkers have openly reverted to an utter value-neutrality.

4 An accessible treatment of the various forms of logical positivism (logical empiricism) and criticism of it is the article by Passmore (1967). On positivism in general, see Abbagnano (1967). The account in the present chapter is based on Holzkamp (1972: 81–85).

5 The present account of falsification theory is based on Holzkamp (1972: 85–89).

6 Implications specifically for the psychology of the human subject will be dealt with in Chapter 4.

7 Neurath, Schlick, and Carnap were prominent members of the neo-positivist Vienna Circle. Neurath was exceptional in his attraction to Marxism. Among other things he attempted to found a 'social behaviourism' based on historical materialism.

8 Loeb was both a socialist and an ardent materialist. He was educated in Germany and taught physiology at the University of Chicago. John B. Watson was one of his students.

9 The account that follows is based on Holzkamp (1984). It is important to acknowledge here that Holzkamp does not claim to have offered a complete critique of phenomenology in general. His remarks were, as noted, directed mainly at Graumann's version, although to the extent that Graumann was true to the phenomenological tradition, Holzkamp's conclusions will apply to it as well. Holzkamp and his colleagues are quick to point out, however, that they have yet to conduct the kind of thorough-going investigation of phenomenology that it clearly deserves.

10 The meaning here is clearer in German: 'into relation' is '*ins Verhältnis*'; 'I relate' is '*ich verhalte mich*', the more common translation of which is 'to act' or 'to behave': thus, putting oneself into relation to the world is to act in the world, which gives 'behaviour' a somewhat richer meaning than is found in behaviourism, where it usually refers simply to passive responding.

11 In the original German this is a play on words. Freedom, says Marx, is not *gegeben* (given), it is *aufgegeben*. The prefix *auf* changes the meaning from simply 'given' to something 'given to do'. The related noun is *Aufgabe* which means 'task' or 'assignment'.

12 The self-identification of dialectical materialism as 'materialism' (apparently initiated by Friedrich Engels) has been a source of trouble from the start. It is an odd designation, given that so much of what the position strives for runs directly counter to the aims of traditional materialism. It was, of course, right to oppose 'idealism', but did that require adoption of the opposite position? That would be very 'undialectical'.

Isn't the position we are talking about really a 'reconciliation' of the opposition between traditional idealism and materialism? After all, as Marx himself began to formulate the position out of his critique of Hegel he did not refer to it as 'materialism', but as 'rational dialectic'.

I think this is an important point, if only because the label has caused Marxism to be confused in many minds, both common and uncommon, with traditional materialism, thus serving as a basis for critique and repudiation on entirely false grounds. Most unfortunately, even Marxists have shared in the confusion, and this contributed substantially to the schematization and dogmatization of dialectical materialism in the 'communist' countries. The matter, therefore, is anything but trivial.

I have personally and lately come to the conclusion that Marxism is not and cannot be 'materialism' in any ordinarily accepted sense (note that Antony Flew had to emphasize the special sense of the word in his entry cited above). This is not the place to give the argument in all the required detail. I think it is worthwhile, however, to make two brief points in substantiation of my concern.

First, the classical Greek philosophers understood the impossibility of the kind of materialism that claims matter to be genetically and logically prior to everything. It was their view that pure matter was utterly inconceivable; we never encounter it in any way but *formed*. Plato responded to this by declaring the priority of form, but Aristotle was more reasonable (dialectical) in giving priority to *substance*, which could be regarded as the unity of matter and form, a position known as *hylomorphism*. If this seems remote from the present issue, consider the following. When I know something, that is, have an idea about it, it is ordinarily not its matter that the idea is about (unless perhaps I am a theoretical physicist), but the form. If matter is always and necessarily encountered only as *formed* matter, and it is its form that my ideas are mainly about (Aristotle believed that ideas were the form of the thing without its matter), it does not seem to make much sense to assert a priority of matter that requires us to deduce our ideas genetically and/or logically from it.

It may be objected that Marx did not have such a purified, abstracted notion of matter in mind. I agree. His idea of matter was very much one of *formed* matter and he well knew that it could only be separated analytically from the idea of it. Exactly! Then why call the position by a label that has a long history of association with the very silliness it opposes?

I am not alone in my concern, but I shall mention here only one prominent ally: Antonio Gramsci, one of the most creative Marxist thinkers of this century, and one who expressed an intense concern for the problems of human subjectivity. His philosophical writings are found mainly in his *Prison Notebooks* (1971) where he referred to Marxism as 'the philosophy of praxis'. Puzzled by this term, some dialectical materialists have maintained that he used it in order to evade the attention of the prison censors. But no one who reads the pertinent texts, even someone with the slightest sophistication about these matters, would be fooled by such a transparent ruse. How could a man as intelligent and clever as Gramsci not have come up with a more effective disguise than this? The answer, I think, is that it was not intended as a disguise but as a correction in terms. His devastating critique of Bukharin's 'Manual' of historical materialism provides ample evidence of his disdain for the mechanical materialism that he found at the heart of Bukharin's work (and which has been reproduced over and over again in official textbooks of dialectical and historical materialism). Gramsci's correction in terminology appears to have been not insignificantly motivated by a need to distance himself from the dogmatic, mechanical Marxists. How else, he might have thought, could he expect to be taken seriously?

I do not propose to correct the terminology in this book. The Critical Psychologists have been content to call themselves 'materialists' and I am not aware that they have had any change of heart on this issue. I think, however, they would, at the very least, insist that we keep in mind that 'materialist' here, as Flew has indicated, has a very special sense that opposes it to traditional materialisms.

3 SOCIAL-HISTORICAL THEORY

1 From the point of view of this distinction, our designation of sociology, anthropology, political economy, history, and psychology as 'social sciences' is a misnomer. Although in German the term *Sozialwissenschaft* is also common, many German 'social scientists' recognize it as implying an unwanted reduction of the societal to the social and would insist on the term *gesellschaftliche Wissenschaft*, or, following the Germanic propensity for compound nouns, *Gesellschaftswissenschaft*. The German for 'society' is *Gesellschaft*.

2 The insistence on maintaining the distinction between *sozial* and *gesellschaftlich*, it should be noted, creates additional problems of translation. For example, while in its adjectival form 'societal' is already awkward, its noun form is even more jarring to Anglophone sensibilities: 'societalness' or 'societality'. (Parenthetically, it should be noted that 'societal nature' might be used in some cases, but only with caution since it tends to presuppose what requires demonstration, that is, that humans are societal by nature. 'Societal character' may rescue us from this problem in some instances.) As if this were not bad enough, we still have to deal with the process of becoming societal: *Vergesellschaftung* = 'societalization'. If we are to preserve the obviously essential distinction between social and societal, I see no way around such seeming barbarities and therefore beg the reader's indulgence. It is entirely conceivable to me that theoretical problems with subjectivity in English-language social science may stem in part from the failure of the language to provide a means of making this distinction more naturally.

3 The word 'nomothetic' is synonymous with 'nomological' and refers to methods, theories, or models that aim to discover or describe general laws. It is contrasted with 'idiographic', which refers to descriptions of individual, concrete cases. The term 'variable-model' is described in the text of this chapter. While the term as we are using it here originates with Holzkamp, it was inspired by an essay on 'sociological analysis and the "variable"' by Herbert Blumer (reprinted in Blumer 1969).

4 The original German text (Marx 1867/1971: 90) uses the term *objektive Gedanken-formen*. The standard English translation (Marx 1867/1906: 87) speaks simply of 'forms of thought expressing with social validity the conditions and relations of a definite, historically determined mode of production.' We follow the original more closely here.

5 The English translation here of *denken in* and *denken über* and related uses of *in* and *über* may, once again, fail to convey fully the meaning intended. Holzkamp (1979: 32), for instance, speaks of societal praxis as thinking-about that leads to acting over and beyond (*über hinaus*) the limits of the exploitive relations represented in the objective thought-forms of bourgeois society. Thinking-about is, therefore, not merely contemplative but a prerequisite for conscious social change. This is an essential contradiction in bourgeois science: it cannot restrict itself entirely to thinking in bourgeois forms if it is to fulfil its scientific mission. It is consequently always pulled in opposing directions and will always pose a *potential* threat to ideological correctness.

4 SPECIFIC PSYCHOLOGICAL THEORIES

1 There is an unquestionable connection between mainstream psychology's devotion to the variable-model (see note 3, Chapter 3) and its positivism. It should be noted, however, that a commitment to a positivist world-view does not commit one at the

same time to the variable-model. The psychologies of Oswald Külpe and Edward Titchener took their inspiration directly from the positivist teachings of Ernst Mach (Danziger 1979), yet they could not be said to represent the variable-model. The aspect of positivism that developed into the variable-model was its emphasis on quantification and measurement (on this see Danziger 1990).

2 That the area of social cognition may not be entirely as bleak as pictured here is indicated by at least one collection of papers published under that title (Damon 1978). The work of Jean Lave (1988) on the 'social anthropology of cognition' can be cited as another bright spot amid the gloom. I think that most of these authors would agree, however, that their thinking is still peripheral to the mainstream, and that their critique of the mainstream shares much in common with that of German Critical Psychology.

5 RECONSTRUCTING THE PSYCHOLOGICAL CATEGORIES

1 The analysis reported by Holzkamp (1983) is one that he had begun earlier (e.g. Holzkamp 1973). Significant contributions to the final result were made by Holzkamp-Osterkamp (1975) and by Schurig (1975a, 1975b, 1976). All these drew significantly, though critically, on earlier work by Leontyev (English translation 1979).

2 It should be noted that when we speak of categories, we shall use the adjective 'categorial' (German: *kategorial*). This word is not found in all English dictionaries, and journal editors persist in altering it to 'categorical' (German: *kategorisch*), the more common meaning of which, in both languages, is 'absolute or unqualified, as in *categorical* denial'. We are deliberately using the word 'categorial' in order to avoid this confusion.

3 Once again, we come to an awkward problem in terminology. In order to talk most generally about that which psychological questions address, it should be clear that words like 'behaviour' and 'cognition' can be misleading. At most they are *expressions* of that which is psychological and should not be equated with it. In the nineteenth century the word 'mind' was often used. Holzkamp and others in his tradition reject this word, however, because it has become so metaphysically burdened by the debates of the last three or four centuries around questions like mind–body dualism. The word 'mental' is similarly burdened. The Greek *psyche* is tempting because it was originally used in a more generalized and descriptive way. Even if we could manage to restore the original Greek usage, however, we would find it too general. After all, Aristotle applied the term as a general principle of life to all living beings including plants. In the meantime, it too has become metaphysically burdened like 'mind' and 'mental'. The German Critical Psychologists, following particular nineteenth-century traditions and, more immediately, the usage established by the cultural-historical school – most particularly A.N. Leontyev – have adopted '*das Psychische*', largely in order to avoid possible substantialist understandings of '*die Psyche*'. This works very well in German, because in that language it achieves the kind of neutrality that is needed. In English, however, this move encounters two problems. First, English converts adjectives into nouns less easily and fluently than German. Second, *das Psychische* can be translated either as 'the psychic' or 'the psychical', both of which have been more or less clearly identified historically with parapsychology. Alas, there is no completely satisfactory solution. The translation of Leontyev's important *Problemy razvitiya psikhiki* (English translation, Leontyev 1981) has, for better or for worse, established a precedent for 'psyche', and I shall adhere to this on the understanding that we want to distinguish it from the 'merely' vital processes. (A definite resemblance to Aristotle's functional usage will be noticed, however: we will simply shift the essential demarcation for 'psyche' from the non-living/living to the non-sentient/sentient.) When the adjectival form is more appropriate, I shall use 'psychical'.

4 'Historical' (German: *historisch*) here means developmental in general, as in the English 'natural history'. It is to be distinguished from 'historical' (German:

geschichtlich) in the human, societal sense, although matters are complicated by the common use in German of the term *Naturgeschichte*.

5 The German here is *autark*, meaning self-sufficient or independent. It is roughly equivalent to 'autonomous'.

6 FROM PHYLOGENESIS TO SOCIOGENESIS

1 This method was characterized as having five steps in Chapter 5. This is always the case when dealing with questions of animal evolution. The fifth step is effectively a return to the first at a new level. With the transition to humans, however, the very nature of further development itself changes (now societal-historical rather than bio-logical-evolutionary). This means that the functional-historical method, which was appropriate to evolutionary development, must now be replaced by more appropriate methods.

2 This is Holzkamp's term (*Erkenntnisdistanz*), and is meant to emphasize the way in which meaning creates a distance between us and the objects of our world, a distance that allows us to 'stand back' and reflect on relations and consequences, make plans, and set goals before acting.

3 The German here is *Handlungsfähigkeit*. *Handlung* means 'action', and *Fähigkeit* is ordinarily translated as 'capability' or simply 'ability'. 'Capacity' is another possi-bility. None of these, the Critical Psychologists maintain, quite grasps their intention. They therefore insist on 'action potence', despite its awkwardness to Anglophone ears.

4 There is, again, something of a translation problem here. Where I am using the word 'control', the Critical Psychologists use *Verfügung über*, which literally means 'disposal over', which approximates the sense of 'subject to one's disposal'. None of the ordinary dictionary meanings of 'disposal', however, quite captures the Critical Psychological intent. It is with some reluctance that I fall back on the more common 'control', which, in English, is subject to overinterpretation, as in the direct control that one might have over a machine. Basically, what is intended is meaningful participation in the decision-making processes that decide our fates.

5 The German here is *Befindlichkeit*. I have not found this in my dictionaries, and my translation of it as 'subjective state' is based on what my German colleagues tell me it means to them. The roots are in the verb *befinden*, which, in the reflexive form, means 'to be' or, more precisely, 'to be situated'. Basically, it is the state I find myself in, as it appears, seems, feels to me.

7 INDIVIDUAL SUBJECTIVITY AND ITS DEVELOPMENT

1 See note 5, Chapter 6.

2 The German here, *Handlungsgründe*, can also be translated as 'reasons for action', but this alternative is rejected owing to its implication of 'rationality', which, by our analysis, remains but a possibility.

3 The reference in this passage to the 'generalized other' will reinforce the sense that some readers will have already that there is a kinship between the work of the German Critical Psychologists and that of George Herbert Mead. I have not encountered any direct references to Mead in the German work. The apparent similarities may be accounted for by the roots common to both positions in the philosophy of Hegel. On the other hand, the work of Herbert Blumer, a student of Mead, has received a critically positive reception by the Berlin group (see Chapter 3).

8 METHODOLOGICAL IMPLICATIONS

1 The use of the designations 'mainstream' and 'bourgeois' here is discussed in the opening paragraphs of Chapter 2.

2 See note 3, Chapter 3.

3 There is, of course, a complicated history of methods in psychology that we cannot rehearse here. The underlying unity of what developed, however, is important for our purposes. It is commonly held that the psychometric tradition based on the development of the correlation coefficient and the experimental tradition based on the t-test and analysis of variance are fundamentally different. This is reflected in numerous debates over correlational versus experimental method, and idiographic versus nomothetic approaches. What all these disputes obscure is the underlying identity of the two methods. Anyone with a modicum of skill at algebra and an understanding of the contents of an elementary statistics textbook can demonstrate for him- or herself that the formulas for t, r, and F (assuming a single degree of freedom in the numerator) are either algebraically equivalent or convertible. A short cut to this insight can be gained by taking tabled critical values of the three statistics to see how they are related. For 1 and 20 degrees of freedom (alpha = 0.05) the value for F is 4.35, for t 2.086. The latter squared yields the former. The critical value for r is 0.4227. That value squared, 0.1787, represents the proportion of variance in the dependent variable related by the regression line to the independent variable. The residual variance, $1 - 0.1787$, divided by the degrees of freedom then becomes a residual 'mean square'. That divided through the proportion of accounted variance, 0.1787, yields 4.35, the value of F. The point is that, at the level of analysis (as opposed to that of hypothesis testing), these methods are essentially identical by virtue of their derivation from the underlying regression analysis, that is, the analysis by which the slope and intercept of the line that best fits the relationship between independent and dependent variables in a bivariate plot is determined. In so far as the wide range of statistical techniques now available is derivative of these, they maintain the underlying unity and universality of the variable model.

4 The use of 'confidence intervals' gives the appearance of yielding positive information. In fact, however, the logic here is identical to that of testing the null hypothesis. The confidence interval merely indicates a range of possible population means (or other statistics) that cannot be rejected on the basis of the characteristics of the sample at hand, given the probability limits that have been more or less arbitrarily specified. Of course, there is a sense in which any negative knowledge implies a positive counterpart. (Ascertaining that my keys are *not* in my pocket implies that they *are* somewhere else. This will, however, offer little consolation if I am locked out of my house.) Several moves have been made recently to increase the appearance of positivity of statistical findings. These include emphases on 'strength of effect' and tests of 'power'. Such moves do add to the yield of information, but they do *not* alter the underlying logic of the null hypothesis test. In the end, the real problem, however, is – as argued elsewhere in this book – the inappropriateness of a methodology that demands the universal application of the variable-model to psychological questions.

5 On the use of 'bourgeois' and 'mainstream', see the second and third paragraphs of Chapter 2.

6 For Hume the 'abstract sciences' included 'politics, natural philosophy, physic, chemistry, &c.'. They were 'abstract' because, unlike the practical sciences like navigation or medicine, they 'treat of general facts' and are not directly concerned with getting a job done. 'Demonstration' refers to the scientific method of inquiry. (See Hume 1777/1966: 182–184.)

7 This is probably more than a mere flirtation. The underlying commonality between positivist-derived philosophical and methodological stances and Platonist

metaphysics has been noted by others. For example, Randall (1962: 32–33) traces the neo-positivist goal of the unity of the sciences based on a reduction of their mathematical laws to a common logic to a similar idea expressed by Plato in *The Republic*.

8 It should be noted that no claim is being made here to have solved the problems historically associated with inductive inference, such as 'affirming the consequent'. Our situation is improved only because we are working from testable categories within a methodological framework that allows generalization to concrete cases.

Further reading

There is relatively little work of the Berlin group that has appeared in English. Klaus Holzkamp's important article on theoretical indeterminacy has been translated (see Holzkamp 1977) and a paper 'on doing psychology critically' has also appeared recently (Holzkamp 1992). The book edited by Tolman and Maiers (1991) contains several contributions by Holzkamp as well as by the present author and several of Holzkamp's colleagues or former students. Wolfgang Maiers has published two important articles in English (1987, 1993). A brief description of the Critical Psychological position that will add nothing to the content of this book was published by the present author (Tolman 1989a). Other papers by the present author (Tolman 1990, 1991b) reflect the influence of Critical Psychology.

A few critical works have appeared in English and should be consulted (Elbers 1987; van Ijzendoorn and van der Veer 1984; and Stroebe 1980).

Critical psychology in its present form shows the significant influence of A.N. Leontyev (Holzkamp's *Grundlegung* is dedicated to his memory). His works (1979, 1981) provide, therefore, some important background. A recent work containing useful discussions of Leontyev's theory has been edited by Lektorsky (1990).

It is important to note that the underlying philosophical assumptions of positions like German Critical Psychology and Leontyev's Activity Theory are quite different from those of Anglophone, academic psychology. Whereas the latter is rooted historically in classical British empiricism, the former find their origins in nineteenth-century German idealism. It is difficult to find accessible discussions of the important differences. One, however, is to be found in an authoritative yet highly readable book by Bakhurst (1991). Chapters 5, 6, and 7 of Bakhurst's book are particularly useful in this regard.

A completely independent, but interestingly similar set of views has recently been published by Lethbridge (1992). This work, in my view, forms an informative and useful comparison to the work of Holzkamp.

Holzkamp's critical approach to the history of psychology is shared by a number of contemporary historians of the discipline. One recent book that readers interested in Critical Psychology will find particularly useful (and compatible with Holzkamp's views, particularly with regard to general methodology and their shared high estimation of the early work of Lewin) is Danziger's *Constructing the Subject* (1990).

References

Abbagnano, N. (1967) 'Positivism' in P. Edwards (ed.) *The Encyclopedia of Philosophy* (Vol. 6: 414–419). New York: Macmillan.

Abercrombie, N., Hill, S., and Turner, B. (1988) *Dictionary of Sociology* (2nd edn). London: Penguin Books.

Alcock, J.E., Carment, D.W., and Sadava, S.W. (1988) *A Textbook of Social Psychology*. Scarborough, Canada: Prentice-Hall.

Arnold, W.J. (1976) 'Introduction' in W.J. Arnold (ed.) *Nebraska Symposium on Motivation 1975*. Lincoln, NE: University of Nebraska.

Ayllon, T., and Azrin, N.H. (1963) 'Intensive treatment of psychotic behavior by stimulus satiation and food reinforcement', *Behavior Research and Therapy*, *1*: 53–61.

Ayllon, T., and Azrin, N.H. (1964) 'The measurement and reinforcement of behavior of psychotics', *Journal of the Experimental Analysis of Behavior*, *8*: 357–383.

Bakhurst, D. (1991) *Consciousness and Revolution in Soviet Philosophy*. Cambridge: Cambridge University Press.

Blumer, H. (1969) *Symbolic Interactionism*. Englewood Cliffs , NJ: Prentice-Hall.

Boring, E.G. (1950) *A History of Experimental Psychology*. New York: Appleton-Century-Crofts.

Braun, K.-H. (1979) *Kritik des Freudo-Marxismus*. Köln: Pahl-Rugenstein.

Braun, K.-H. (1991) 'Play and ontogenesis' in C.W. Tolman and W. Maiers (eds) *Critical Psychology: Contributions to an Historical Science of the Subject* (pp. 212–233). New York: Cambridge University Press.

Carr, H.A. (1925) *Psychology*. New York: Longmans, Green & Co.

Catania, A.C. (1973) 'The psychologies of structure, function and development', *American Psychologist*, *28*: 434–443.

Coser, L.A. (1977) *Masters of Sociological Thought* (2nd edn). New York: Harcourt Brace Jovanovich.

Damon, W. (1978) *Social Cognition*. San Francisco: Jossey-Bass.

Danziger, K. (1979) 'The positivist repudiation of Wundt', *Journal of the History of the Behavioural Sciences*, *15*: 205–230.

Danziger, K. (1983) 'Origins and basic principles of Wundt's *Völkerpsychologie*', *British Journal of Social Psychology*, *22*: 303–313.

Danziger, K. (1990) *Constructing the Subject: Historical Origins of Psychological Research*. Cambridge: Cambridge University Press.

de Rivera, J. (1976) *Field Theory as Human Science: Contributions of Lewin's Berlin Group*. New York: Gardner.

Dollard, J., and Miller, N.E. (1950) *Personality and Psychotherapy*. New York: McGraw-Hill.

'Dr. crit.' (1967) *Der Spiegel*, 24 July: 36.

Dreier, O. (1980) *Familiäres Sein und familiäres Bewusstsein: Therapeutische Analyse einer Arbeiterfamilie*. Frankfurt/Main: Campus Verlag.

Dreier, O. (1991) 'Client interests and possibilities in psychotherapy' in C.W. Tolman and W. Maiers (eds) *Critical Psychology: Contributions to an Historical Science of the Subject* (pp. 196–211). New York: Cambridge University Press.

Elbers, E. (1987) 'Critical psychology and the development of motivation as historical process' in J.M. Broughton (ed.) *Critical Theories of Psychological Development* (pp. 149–175). New York: Plenum Press.

Elms, A.C. (1975) 'The crisis of confidence in social psychology', *American Psychologist, 30*: 967–976.

English, H.B., and English, A.C. (1958) *A Comprehensive Dictionary of Psychological and Psychoanalytic Terms*. New York: Longmans, Green & Co.

Flanagan, O.J. (1984) *The Science of the Mind*. Cambridge, MA: MIT Press.

Flew, A. (1979) *A Dictionary of Philosophy*. London: Pan Books/Macmillan.

Freud, S. (1973) *The Future of an Illusion*. London: The Hogarth Press. (Original work published 1927.)

Freud, S. (1975) *Civilization and Its Discontents*. London: The Hogarth Press. (Original work published 1930.)

Freund, J. (1969) *The Sociology of Max Weber*. New York: Vintage Books.

Gleiss, I. (1975) 'Verhalten oder Tätigkeit', *Kritische Psychologie (I)*. Berlin: Argument-Verlag.

Gleitman, H. (1991) *Psychology* (3rd edn). New York: W.W. Norton & Co.

Gramsci, A. (1971) *Selections from the Prison Notebooks* (edited and translated by Q. Hoare and G.N. Smith). New York: International Publishers.

Graumann, C.F. (1984) 'Phänomenologische Analytik und experimentelle Methodik in der Psychologie: Das Problem ihrer Vermittlung', paper read at the 3rd International Congress for Critical Psychology, Marburg, 11–12 May.

Hall, C.S. (1955) *A Primer of Freudian Psychology*. New York: New American Library.

Hamlyn, D.W. (1967) 'History of epistemology' in P. Edwards (ed.) *The Encyclopedia of Philosophy* (Vol. 3: 8–38). New York: Macmillan.

Harré, R., and Secord, P.F. (1972) *The Explanation of Behaviour*. Oxford: Basil Blackwell.

Haug, W.F. (1977) 'Bürgerliche Privatform des Individuums und Umweltform der Gesellschaft' in K.-H. Braun and K. Holzkamp (eds) *Kritische Psychologie*. Köln: Pahl-Rugenstein.

Heidbreder, E. (1933) *Seven Psychologies*. New York: Appleton-Century.

Hilgard, E.R. (1987) *Psychology in America: A Historical Survey*. New York: Harcourt Brace Jovanovich.

Hilgard, E.R., and Bower, G.H. (1966) *Theories of Learning*. New York: Appleton-Century-Crofts.

Holzkamp, K. (1964) *Theorie und Experiment in der Psychologie*. Berlin: DeGruyter.

Holzkamp, K. (1968) *Wissenschaft als Handlung*. Berlin: DeGruyter.

Holzkamp, K. (1972) *Kritische Psychologie: Vorbereitende Arbeiten*. Frankfurt/M.: Fischer-Verlag.

Holzkamp, K. (1973) *Sinnliche Erkenntnis: Historischer Ursprung und gesellschaftliche Funktion der Wahrnehmung*. Königstein/Ts.: Athenäum-Verlag.

Holzkamp, K. (1977) 'Die Überwindung der wissenschaftlichen Beliebigkeit psychologischer Theorien durch die Kritische Psychologie', *Zeitschrift für Sozialpsychologie, 8*: 1–22, 78–79. [Reprinted in Holzkamp 1978; a shortened English translation by L. Zusne appears in R. Hogan and W. Jones (eds) *Perspectives in Personality* (Vol. 2: 93–123), Greenwich, CT: JAI Press.]

Holzkamp, K. (1978) *Gesellschaftlichkeit des Individuums*. Köln: Pahl-Rugenstein.

Holzkamp, K. (1979) 'Zur kritisch-psychologischen Theorie der Subjektivität I: Das Verhältnis von Subjektivität und Gesellschaftlichkeit in der traditionellen Sozialwissenschaft und im Wissenschaftlichen Sozialismus', *Forum Kritische Psychologie*, Nr. 4: 10–54.
Holzkamp, K. (1983) *Grundlegung der Psychologie*. Frankfurt/M.: Campus Verlag.
Holzkamp, K. (1984) 'Kritische Psychologie und phänomenologische Psychologie: Der Weg der Kritischen Psychologie zur Subjektwissenschaft', *Forum Kritische Psychologie*, Nr. 14: 5–55.
Holzkamp, K. (1985) 'Zur Stellung der Psychoanalyse in the Geschichte der Psychologie' in K.-H. Braun, O. Dreier, W. Hollitscher, K. Holzkamp, M. Markard, G. Minz, and K. Wetzel (eds) *Geschichte und Kritik der Psychoanalyse* (pp. 13–69). Marburg: Verlag Arbeiterbewegung und Gesellschaftswissenschaft.
Holzkamp, K. (1991a) 'Experience of self and scientific objectivity' in C.W. Tolman and W. Maiers (eds) *Critical Psychology: Contributions to an Historical Science of the Subject*. New York: Cambridge University Press. (Originally published as 'Selbsterfahrung und wissenschaftliche Objektivität' in *Subjektivität als Problem psychologischer Methodik*. Frankfurt/M: Campus Verlag, 1984.)
Holzkamp, K. (1991b) 'Psychoanalysis and Marxist psychology' in C.W. Tolman and W. Maiers (eds) *Critical Psychology: Contributions to an Historical Science of the Subject*. New York: Cambridge University Press. (Originally published as 'Die Bedeutung der Freudschen Psychoanalyse für die marxistisch fundierte Psychologie' in *Forum Kritische Psychologie*, Nr. 13, 1984.)
Holzkamp, K. (1992) 'On doing psychology critically', *Theory and Psychology*, 2: 193–204.
Holzkamp. K. (1993) *Lernen: Subjektwissenschaftliche Grundlegung*. Frankfurt/M: Campus Verlag.
Holzkamp-Osterkamp, U. (1975) *Grundlagen der psychologischen Motivationsforschung 1*. Frankfurt/M: Campus Verlag.
Holzkamp-Osterkamp, U. (1976) *Motivationsforschung 2: Die Besonderung menschlicher Bedürfnisse – Problematik und Erkenntnisgehalt der Psychoanalyse*. Frankfurt/M: Campus Verlag.
Hume, D. (1966) *An Enquiry Concerning Human Understanding*. La Salle, IL: Open Court. (Original work published 1777.)
Jaeggi, E. (1975) 'Persönlichkeitstheoretische Implikationen verhaltenstherapeutischer Praxis', *Kritische Psychologie (I)*. Berlin: Argument-Verlag.
Jäger, M., Kersten, K., Leiser, E., Maschewsky, W., and Schneider, U. (1979) *Subjektivität als Methodenproblem*. Köln: Pahl-Rugenstein.
Kant, I. (1970) *Metaphysical Foundations of Natural Science*. Indianapolis: Bobbs-Merrill. (Original work published 1786.)
'Knüppel frei' (1967) *Der Spiegel*, 12 June: 41–46.
Lave, J. (1988) *Cognition in Practice*. New York: Cambridge University Press.
Lektorsky, V.A. (ed.) (1990) *Activity: The Theory, Methodology and Problems*. Orlando, FA: Paul M. Deutsch Press.
Leontyev, A.N. (1979) *Problems of the Development of the Mind*. Moscow: Progress Publishers.
Leontyev, A.N. (1981) 'The problem of activity in psychology' in J. Wertsch (ed.) *The Concept of Activity in Soviet Psychology* (pp. 37–71). Armonk, NY: Sharpe.
Lethbridge, D. (1992) *Mind in the World: The Marxist Psychology of Self-Actualization*. Minneapolis: MEP Publications.
Lewin, K. (1931) 'The conflict between Aristotelian and Galileian modes of thought in contemporary psychology', *Journal of Genetic Psychology*, 5: 141–177.
Lorenz, K. (1965) *Evolution and the Modification of Behavior*. Chicago: University of Chicago Press.

McLellan, D. (1991) 'What is living and what is dead in Marxism?', *The Month*, April: 138–143.

Maiers, W. (1975) 'Normalität und Pathologie des Psychischen', *Kritische Psychologie (1)*. Berlin: Argument-Verlag.

Maiers, W. (1987) 'The historical approach of critical psychology: another case of paradigm shift?' in W. Baker, M. Hyland, H. Rappard, and A. Staats (eds) *Current Issues in Theoretical Psychology* (pp. 175-188). Amsterdam: North-Holland.

Maiers, W. (1988). 'Has psychology exaggerated its "natural scientific character"?' in W. Baker, L. Mos, H. Rappard, and H. Stam (eds) *Recent Trends in Theoretical Psychology* (pp. 133–143). New York: Springer-Verlag.

Maiers, W. (1993) 'Psychological theorizing in a subject-scientific perspective: determining subjective grounds for action' in H. Stam, L. Mos, W. Thorngate and B. Kaplan (eds) *Recent Trends in Psychological Theory* (Vol. 3). New York: Springer-Verlag.

Marx, K. (1906) *Capital* (Vol. 1). Chicago: Charles H. Kerr. (Original work published 1867.)

Marx, K. (1909) *Capital* (Vol. 3). Chicago: Charles H. Kerr. (Original work published 1894.)

Marx, K. (1971) *Das Kapital* (Vol. 1). Berlin: Dietz Verlag. (Original work published 1867.)

Marx, K., and Engels, F. (1970) *The German Ideology*. New York: International Publishers. (Original work published 1846.)

Moscovici, S. (1972) 'Society and theory in social psychology' in J. Israel and H. Tajfel (eds) *The Context of Social Psychology* (pp. 17–68). New York: Academic Press.

'Nein, nein, nein' (1967) *Der Spiegel*, 5 June: 46–59.

Passmore, J. (1967) 'Logical positivism' in P. Edwards (ed.) *The Encyclopedia of Philosophy* (Vol. 5: 52–57). New York: Macmillan.

Popper, K.R. (1961) *The Logic of Scientific Discovery*. New York: Science Editions.

Popper, K.R. (1966) *Logik der Forschung* (2nd edn). Tübingen: Unbekannter Verlag.

Randall, J.H., Jr. (1962) *Aristotle*. New York: Columbia University Press.

Reich, W. (1963) *The Sexual Revolution*. New York: Farrar, Straus & Cudahy.

Rogers, T.B. (1991) 'Antecedents of operationism: a case history in radical positivism' in C.W. Tolman (ed.) *Positivism in Psychology: Historical and Contemporary Problems*. New York: Springer-Verlag.

Schurig, V. (1975a) *Naturgeschichte des Psychischen 1: Psychogenese und elementare Formen der Tierkommunikation*. Frankfurt/M: Campus.

Schurig, V. (1975b) *Naturgeschichte des Psychischen 2: Lernen und Abstraktionsleistungen bei Tieren*. Frankfurt/M: Campus.

Schurig, V. (1976) *Die Entstehung des Bewusstseins*. Frankfurt/M: Campus.

'Sehr heiss' (1967) *Der Spiegel*, 3 July: 26.

Shepard, R.N., and Metzler, J. (1971) 'Mental rotation of three-dimensional objects' in *Science, 171*: 81–106.

Skinner, B.F. (1948) *Walden Two*. New York: Macmillan.

Skinner, B.F. (1953) *Science and Human Behavior*. New York: Macmillan.

Skinner, B.F. (1956) 'A case history in scientific method', *American Psychologist, 11*: 221–233.

Smythe, W.E. (1991) 'Positivism and the prospects for cognitive science' in C.W. Tolman (ed.) *Positivism in Psychology: Historical and Contemporary Problems*. New York: Springer-Verlag.

Staats, A.W. (1983) *Psychology's Crisis of Disunity: Philosophy and Method for Unified Science*. New York: Praeger.

Staeuble, I. (1968) 'Faschistoide und kritisch-autonome Haltung. Versuch über die Rolle des Konzepts "Einstellung zu kritischer Vernunft" in der Vorurteilsforschung', *Zeitschrift für Soziologie und Sozialpsychologie, 20*: 38–61.

Stivers, E., and Wheelan, S. (1986) *The Lewin Legacy: Field Theory in Current Practice.*
Berlin: Springer-Verlag.

Stroebe, W. (1980) 'The critical school in German social psychology', *Personality and Social Psychology Bulletin,* 6: 105–112.

Tent, J.F. (1988) *The Free University of Berlin: A Political History.* Bloomington, IN: Indiana University Press.

Tolman, C.W. (1988) 'Theoretical unification in psychology: a materialist perspective' in W.J. Baker, L.P. Mos, H.V. Rappard, and H.J. Stam (eds) *Recent Trends in Theoretical Psychology.* New York: Springer-Verlag.

Tolman, C.W. (1989a) 'What's critical about Kritische Psychologie?', *Canadian Psychology,* 30: 628–635.

Tolman, C.W. (1989b) 'The general psychological crisis and its comparative psychological resolution', *The International Journal of Comparative Psychology,* 2: 197–209.

Tolman, C.W. (1990) 'For a materialist psychology' in W. Baker, M. Hyland, R. van Hezewijk, and S. Terwee (eds) *Recent Trends in Theoretical Psychology, Vol. 2.* New York: Springer-Verlag.

Tolman, C.W. (1991a) 'Neopositivism and perception theory' in C.W. Tolman (ed.) *Positivism in Psychology: Historical and Contemporary Problems.* New York: Springer-Verlag.

Tolman, C.W. (1991b) 'Theoretical indeterminacy, pluralism, and the conceptual concrete', *Theory and Psychology,* 1: 147–162.

Tolman, C.W. (1991c) 'Watson's positivism: materialism or phenomenalism?' in C.W. Tolman (ed.) *Positivism in Psychology: Historical and Contemporary Problems.* New York: Springer-Verlag.

Tolman, C.W., and Maiers, W. (1991) (eds) *Critical Psychology: Contributions to an Historical Science of the Subject.* New York: Cambridge University Press.

'Urteil im Zwielicht' (1967) *Der Spiegel,* 27 November: 74.

van Ijzendoorn, M.H., and van der Veer, R. (1984) *Main Currents of Critical Psychology.* New York: Irvington.

Vygotsky, L.S. (1978) *Mind in Society.* Cambridge, MA: Harvard University Press.

Warhaft, S. (1965) *Francis Bacon: A Selection of His Works.* Toronto: Macmillan.

Watson, J.B. (1930) *Behaviorism.* New York: Norton.

Weber, S.J., and Cook, T.D. (1972) 'Subject effects in laboratory research: an examination of subject roles, demand characteristics, and valid inference', *Psychological Bulletin,* 77: 273–295.

'Wir fordern die Enteignung Axel Springers' (1967) *Der Spiegel,* 10 July: 29–33.

Wolpoff, M.H. (1980) *Paleoanthropology.* New York: Knopf.

Wright, R.V.S. (1972) 'Imitative learning of a flaked stone technology: the case of an orangutan', *Mankind,* 8: 296–306.

Name index

Subject index